Bastille Nation

French Penal Politics and the Punitive Turn

Jean Bérard and Gilles Chantraine

Translated from the French by
Matthew Cunningham

RED QUILL BOOKS

© Red Quill Books Ltd. 2013
Ottawa

www.redquillbooks.com
ISBN 978-1-926958-22-4

Printed on acid-free paper. The paper used in this book incorporates post-consumer waste and has not been sourced from endangered old growth forests, forests of exceptional conservation value or the Amazon Basin. Red Quill Books subscribes to a one-book-at-a-time manufacturing process that substantially lessens supply chain waste, reduces greenhouse emissions, and conserves valuable natural resources.

Library and Archives Canada Cataloguing in Publication

Bastille nation : French penal politics and the punitive turn / by Jean Bérard and Gilles Chantraine ; translated by Matthew Cunningham.

Includes bibliographical references.
ISBN 978-1-926958-22-4

1. Prison administration—France. 2. Criminal justice, Administration of—France. 3. Prisons—Law and legisla-tion—France. 4. Prisoners—Legal status, laws, etc.—France. 5. France—Politics and government—21st century. I. Chantraine, Gilles II. Title. III. Title: French penal politics and the punitive turn.

HV9667.B47 2013   365'.944   C2013-900551-X

This book is a substantially re-written, updated and translated version of: *80 000 détenus en 2017? : Réforme et dérive de l'institution pénitentiaire* Published by Éditions Amsterdam, 2008.

RQB is a radical publishing house.
Part of the proceeds from the sale of this book will support student scholarships.

ACKNOWLEDGEMENTS

Behind the signature on every book hide accomplices, colleagues, publishers and friends. This work would not exist without the journal Vacarme, which gave our first reflections a special place for discussion and publication. Our work would not have undergone a first phase of construction and synthesis without the help of Éditions Amsterdam. Finally, it would have had many more imperfections without Nicolas Carrier, Joël Charbit, George Rigakos, Hugues de Suremain, Grégory Salle and Loïc Wacquant and the evaluators at Red Quill Books, who agreed to comment on the first versions of this text. To all of them we express our most heartfelt thanks, as well as to our translator, Matthew Cunningham. The errors and omissions that remain are, quite obviously, our own.

BASTILLE NATION: FRENCH PENAL POLITICS AND THE PUNITIVE TURN

TABLE OF CONTENTS

GLOSSARY

ADDD: *Association pour la défense des droits des détenus* (Association for the Defence of Prisoners' Rights).

CAP: *Comité d'action des prisonniers* (Prisoners' Action Committee). A protest movement born in 1972, active until the early 1980s. Founded by former prisoners, taking over from *Groupe d'information sur les prisons* (see GIP). Very active in the fight against high-security wings.

CCAS: *Centre communal d'action sociale* (Community Centre for Social Action). A public community establishment that is mainly involved in social security and running social programs.

CEF: *Centre éducatif fermé* (closed education centre). CEFs house multiple-offence juvenile delinquents aged 13 to 18. The system is presented as an educational alternative to detention. CEFs are also characterized by legal confinement. A minor who fails to respect CEF conditions or the obligations established by a court decision may be placed in detention.

CER: *Centre éducatif renforcé* (reinforced education centre). These organizations are part of the *Protection Judiciaire de la Jeunesse* (Youth Judicial Protection Service). They have the authority to take charge of multiple-offence juvenile delinquents who have serious financial difficulties or are on the road to marginalization. Many of them have a long history with instututions.

CGLPL: *Contrôleur général des lieux de privation de liberté* (General Inspector of All Places of Deprivation of Liberty). Instituted by law no. 2007- 1545 of 30 October 2007, the CGLPL ensures that those deprived of liberty are treated humanely and with respect for the dignity inherent to human beings, through visits, reports and recommendations.

CGT: *Confédération générale du travail* (General Labour Confederation). Employee union founded in 1895.

CHRS: *Centre d'hébergement et de réinsertion sociale* (emergency accommodation and social rehabilitation centre). This is a category of establishments working in the area of accommodation and social and professional rehabilitation for people in situations of social exclusion.

CHU: *Centre d'hébergement d'urgence* (emergency accommodation centre). An establishment that offers a few nights of accommodation to the homeless. Usually managed by non-profit organizations.

CNCDH: *Commission nationale consultative des droits de l'homme* (The French National Consultative Commission on Human Rights). This commission advises the government and makes proposals in the areas of human rights, law, humanitarian action and respect for the fundamental guarantees protecting citizens' right to exercise public freedoms.

CNDS: *Commission nationale de déontologie de la sécurité* (National Commission on Ethics and Security). An independent administrative authority created in 2000, responsible for monitoring the legality of the behaviour of public employees in law enforcement and the justice system.

CPT: European Committee for the Prevention of Torture. Established by the Council of Europe's "European Convention for the Prevention of Torture and Inhuman or Degrading Treatment or Punishment", it entered into force in 1989. The CPT is a preventative, non-judicial mechanism to protect people deprived of liberty against torture and all other mistreatment.

CS: Correctional Service (*administration pénitentiaire*). A department within the Ministry of Justice responsible for people placed under the authority of the justice system.

CSA: Correctional Service administration (*direction de l'administration pénitentiaire*). See CS.

DQ: Disciplinary wings. Wings in which the harshest disciplinary sanctions are served in jail.

ECHR: The European Court of Human Rights is a supranational jurisdictional body created by the European Convention on Human Rights in the context of the Council of Europe. Its mission is to safeguard human rights and fundamental freedoms. The European Court of Human Rights has jurisdiction when a Council of Europe member state that has ratified the Convention fails to respect the rights and freedoms it recognizes. Created in 1959.

EPR: European Prison Rules. A set of detailed prescriptions relating to prisons, published by the Council of Europe. A new version was passed on 11 January 2006. They are intended for all Council of Europe member states, but are not binding.

ERIS: *Équipes régionales d'intervention et de sécurité* (regional response and security teams). Correctional Service response teams, created in 2003.

FN: *Front national* (National Front). Extreme right-wing political party.

FNARS: *Fédération nationale des associations d'accueil et de réinsertion sociale* (National Federation of Social Rehabilitation Associations). A group of associations that help people in situations of social exclusion.

GIGN: *Groupes d'intervention de la gendarmerie nationale* (National Gendarmerie Response Teams). A unit of the French national Gendarmerie that specializes in counter-terrorism and hostage liberation operations.

GIP: *Groupe Information Prison* (Prison Information Group). An action and information movement created after the 8 February 1971 manifesto signed by Jean-Marie Domenach, Michel Foucault and Pierre Vidal-Naquet, with the goal of enabling prisoner expression and the mobilization of intellectuals and professionals involved with the prison system.

GIPN: *Groupes d'intervention de la police nationale* (National Police Response Teams). French national police units, regionally assigned, called to intervene in hostage-takings, terrorist acts, prison revolts or the questioning of deranged individuals.

GMP: *Groupe Multiprofessionnel des Prisons* (Prisons Multiprofessional Group). An activist group founded in the 1970s whose members either work in prisons or are connected to the prison system.

INSEE: *Institut national de la statistique et des études économiques* (National Institute of Statistics and Economic Studies). Responsible for producing, analyzing and distributing official statistics in France.

JAP: *Juge de l'application des peines* (Penalty Enforcement Judge). A specialized regional court judge responsible for keeping track of convicts inside and outside prison. According to article 712-1 of the Code of Criminal Procedure, "the penalty enforcement judge and the penalty enforcement court constitute the first level of courts for the application of sentences, which are responsible for determining the main conditions for implementing custodial sentences, and certain other penalties restrictive of liberty, by directing and overseeing the conditions of their execution".

IPW: *Observatoire international des prisons - section française* (International Prison Watch - French Section). An association founded in 1996, which aims to raise awareness about the prison situation and promote prisoner rights.

PCF: *Parti communiste français* (French Communist Party)

PS: *Parti socialiste* (Socialist Party)

QHS: *Quartier haute sécurité* (high-security wings). This acronym groups together QSRs (*quartiers de sécurité renforcée* / increased security wings) and QPGSs (*quartiers de plus grande sécurité* / highest-security wings). Instituted in the 1970s and abolished in the early 1980s.

RSA: *Revenu de solidarité active* (active solidarity revenue). A social welfare payment intended to guarantee beneficiaries, whether they are able to work or not, a minimum revenue. It was experimented in 34 counties beginning in May 2007, and rolled out nationally beginning on 1 June 2009. It replaced the RMI (*revenu minimum d'insertion* / minimum integration revenue), and is different in that it offers the beneficiary the possibility of retaining part of the allowance when he or she resumes part-time work.

RSC: Restricted Steering Committee (*Comité d'orientation restreint*), responsible for preparing the penitentiary reform.

SAMU: *Service d'aide médicale urgente* (emergency medical service). The response service for medical emergencies (road accidents, etc.).

SDF: Sans domicile fixe (with no fixed address). This has become the most common way of referring to homeless people administratively, politically and in the media.

SPIP: *Service pénitentiaire d'insertion et de probation* (Rehabilitation and Parole Services). This service is responsible for prisoner rehabilitation and tracking people on probation in "open custody".

UDF: *Union pour la démocratie française* (Union for French Democracy). Centre-right political party.

UHSA: *Unité hospitalière spécialement aménagée* (Specially Equipped Hospital Wards). Wards designed for the care of prisoners with psychiatric disorders. The first of these wards opened in Lyon in 2010.

UMD: *Unité pour malades difficiles* (Wards for Difficult Patients). Psychiatric medical service specializing in the treatment of mentally ill patients considered to be dangerous.

UMP: *Union pour un mouvement populaire* (Union for a Popular Movement). Right-wing political party.

UVF: *Unité de visite familiale* (family visit unit). Enables incarcerated individuals to meet their close relations and share moments of privacy for several hours without supervision. More specifically, a UVF is a furnished apartment situated within the prison's outer walls, but outside the detention area. The first UVF opened in 2004.

The principal types of penitentiary custodial establishments in France

1/ JAILS

A jail (*maison d'arrêt*) is where provisional detention is executed (detained persons awaiting judgement). It also houses convicts who are not serving a "long sentence", whose minimum terms do not, theoretically, exceed two years at the time of conviction.

2/ PENAL ESTABLISHMENTS

Penal establishments (*établissements pour peine*) are prisons housing people sentenced by the criminal courts. There are several types:

Detention centres (*centres de détention*) house prisoners considered to have the best rehabilitation prospects. To this end, detention centres are theoretically a detention regime that is mainly oriented towards prisoner "resocialization".

Prisons (maisons centrales) house convicts who are considered the most difficult and whose rehabilitation prospects are most remote. It is in prisons that security systems are most important.

Penitentiary centres (*centres pénitentiaires*) are mixed establishments comprising at least two wings enforcing different detention regimes (jail, detention centre and/or prison).

Semi-release centres (*centres de semi-liberté*) house convicts admitted to the external placement regime without surveillance, or the semi-release regime. The detained convict can leave the custodial establishments to engage in a professional activity, receive schooling or training, or receive medical treatment.

Prisons for minors (*établissements pénitentiaires pour mineurs*) only house detained minors (either convicted or awaiting judgement). The detained minors can also be incarcerated in special wings for minors situated within jails.

INTRODUCTION

This book tells the story of an attempt to reform the French prison system, resulting in the passing of a penitentiary law at the end of 2009. This law had been ten years in the making, and was presented as the culmination of the modernization and humanization of the French carceral system. In 2000, a doctor published a book that exposed the scandalous state of French prisons (Vasseur 2000), bringing the carceral system under the media spotlight. The daily newspaper *Le Monde* published extracts from the book describing catastrophic detention conditions at La Santé Jail in Paris. These sparked a wave of indignation. MPs from both chambers led an inquiry into the carceral system, vigorously denouncing a situation that was "humiliating" for the French Republic (Mermaz and Floch 2000; Hyest and Cabanel 2000). Reform was placed on the agenda.

But this reform, which should have responded urgently to a situation universally regarded as unacceptable, was not to be passed for another ten years. Legislation was drafted in 2000-2001 and then abandoned when the right wing was placing violence at the heart of the 2002 presidential campaign. Discussion of the new law ceased entirely from 2002 to 2007. After once again being promised by all candidates in the 2007 presidential campaign, the reform followed a turbulent trajectory. It was tabled by a Minister who was quickly thrown into disgrace[1], then completed by a Minister who was quickly called away to other govern-

---

1   Rachida Dati, Minister of Justice from May 2007 to June 2009.

ment duties[2], then drafted by a Correctional Service director who left his post a few weeks after the vote[3]. The legislation travelled a rocky road through Parliament. A law was eventually passed without haste and without raising hopes of significant changes to the conditions governing both prisoners and prison Correctional Service officials.

One fundamental reason for this scepticism was the fact that France's carceral population had been soaring since the early 2000s. In July 2004, the number of people incarcerated in France reached 64,000, a figure unheard of since the end of the Second World War. In December 2011 it attained a record level of 65,200 prisoners, whereas the figure was 48,216 in 2001 and 38,639 in 1980. At the beginning of 2011, the number of people in detention, including those required to wear an electronic bracelet, surpassed 70,000—another unprecedented figure.

By an overwhelming majority, the carceral population continues to be made up of young men in very precarious social situations. But the grounds and duration of incarceration have changed dramatically: the number of admissions has fluctuated significantly (falling between 1980 and 2002); the number of people being monitored in "open custody" has increased (142,000 in 2007, 168,000 in 2010); the average duration of incarceration has risen from 4 to 9.4 months (Tournier 2011a; Tournier 2011b); a growing percentage of the population is being convicted for attacks against people (especially sexual offences); the carceral population is aging relatively, etc.

In this context, the reform was subjected to several re-writes, laborious negotiations and much criticism, demonstrating the contradictions that ensnare any attempt to reform the prison system. The government was establishing new institutions to control prisons while at the same time trying to retain the Correctional Service's discretionary power. It claimed that prisoners' rights should be recognised while

---

2   Michèle Alliot-Marie, from June 2009 to November 2010.
3   Claude D'Harcourt, dismissed from his post in January 2010. The law had finally been passed in November 2009.

implementing detention regimes that created the possibility of controlling the exercise of these rights. The Ministry of Justice had to defend its *expertise monopoly*. This was challenged by other political actors: opposition political parties, unions and associations, as well as public institutions responsible for drafting human rights proposals. Analysing this conflict is one of the central threads of our text.

However, the book also aims to contribute to the study of the various means by which prisoners make demands and subjectify themselves. In this sense, it recounts the history of prisons "on the outside" as well as "on the inside". Like other exceptionally restrictive institutions, prison is a place where one can observe a concentrated manifestation of the conflict between the voices of the dominated and the dominators's power to deal with these voices. Between noise and words (Rancière 1995), between hidden transcripts and public performances (Scott 1990), the words of the dominated get trampled under a political subjection strategy. With the exception of a few prisons, all collective expression by prisoners is strictly prohibited in France. It can therefore only exist as transgressions that are always liable to be repressed. When the institution *asks the prisoners to speak*, it does so either in the spirit of limited participation in the organization of everyday pastimes—something that excludes all issues that generate anger—or in the spirit of an injunction to "take ownership" of the execution of one's own penalty. In short, when the institution encourages prisoners to speak, though the aim might be to make social relations more fluid and penological pretensions more sophisticated, the intention is certainly not to treat prisoners as political subjects. Consequently, the grounds for prisoner and staff dissatisfaction have not disappeared, but as issues they struggle to enter the public debate.

To hear a quite different story, it is enough to create a forum outside the *in camera* between prisoners and the Correctional Service. This was demonstrated in a 1967 work that describes a support group experiment initiated in 1962 by the doctor and psychotherapist Daniel Gonin. Participants were able to express themselves very freely because "the counselor answers questions but does not direct". From the outset, there were complaints about day-to-day prison life. These initially focused on hygiene (Gonin 1967)[4]. Then the group turned their attention to the core of prison repression: the guards' ability to report undisciplined behaviour, and more particularly the director's disciplinary authority: "Some of them seem decent, they chat with you. But then they go to the head guard and run you down behind your back. Some of them try to get you to be rude by treating you like an idiot... and if they can even get you to hit them... They'd be more than happy to give the other guards a reason to smash your head in. You'd get reported and you'd tend to your wounds in solitary. That's how they're trained"; "And the director who sends you to court won't listen to you. He'll read a badly-written report, not even proper French, he'll take the guard's word. You're never allowed to say anything and if you try to speak, you get fifteen more days. He's satisfied, he's done his bit of justice". After expressing their disapproval of prison power relationships, the support group attacked the operation of the penal justice system, first by questioning the validity of assessments: "in half an hour, how can a doctor, even a psychiatrist, know everything about you, not only seeing into your past but even predicting your future, what will become of you in ten or twenty years, whether or not you'll be beyond rehabilitation?"; "It was even worse for me. He said: 'haven't you ever felt the desire to sleep with your mother?' Can you imagine? He was lucky we weren't on the outside".

This brief attempt to place in perspective the points of view of the disciplinarians and those they discipline reveals a discrepancy that says something about how the 2009 penitentiary law was created. The Correctional Service saw the reform as the process of updating legal data relating to the prison situation. The minister explained that it must "give the Correctional Service a regulatory framework that trans-

---

4   The quotations in this paragraph have been taken from the body of this text.

lates the advances of the past twenty years"[5]. Translating "the advances of the past twenty years" was just another way of saying that nothing fundamental had to be changed in terms of prisoners' rights. They only needed to formulate the correct interlinking between penitentiary assessment structures and legal provisions relating to prisoner classification and placement[6]. The prisoners' opinion of the crushing power relationships to which they would be subjected under these new forms of management was simply not considered. That being said, the situation has changed significantly since the 1960s. Prisons have opened to outside contributors; they have been the subject of political debate and media coverage; they are required to at least partly submit to independent checks; they are challenged through the courts by associations. In other words, prison discourse is no longer solely limited to official government texts and the criticism of the people who are confined within the walls of prisons.

To reconstruct the complexity of the struggles and controversies that surround the French prison system, it is first necessary to outline the distinctive characteristics of a field of activism and politics that involves not just French actors, but also European authorities. Within the Ministry of Justice, the *Correctionnal Service Administration* is responsible for people who have been placed under the control of the justice system, in prison or in open custody. The Correctional Service (CS) is one of the central characters in our story. Other official authorities play a role as well. Some are European, aiming to evaluate the application of the *European Convention on Human Rights* as well as recommendations drawn up by the *Council of Europe*, specifically their *European Prison Rules*. When there exists no recourse to national law, or when all of its avenues have been exhausted, cases can be referred to *The European Court of Human Rights*. The *European Committee for the Prevention of Torture* (CPT) and the *European Commissioner of Human Rights* make periodic visits, writing reports and making recommendations. Other authorities are French, such

---

5   Administration pénitentiaire, *Chiffres clefs 2007 - Perspectives 2008*, 22 February 2008.
6   See chapter 3.

as the *National Consultative Commission on Human Rights* (CNCDH[7]), composed of qualified figures and representatives from civil society who recommend legislation. More recent is the *General Inspector of All Places of Deprivation of Liberty*, an independent administrative authority established in 2008[8] that also visits places of detention and draws up recommendations. From 2000 until its dissolution in 2011, the *National Commission on Ethics and Security* (*Commission nationale de déontologie de la sécurité*, or CNDS)[9] investigated cases of abuse by police[10]. These authorities work in conjunction with associations and researchers, specifically to supply international comparative data. Activists regularly present secondary expert assessments to highlight abuses by the CS and debunk its portrayal of the prison situation. This is particularly the case for the French section of *International Prison Watch* (IPW). Activists rely on the documents and recommendations of official authorities to evaluate government policy and make it available to the public. One of their tasks is to make sure that these official reports find their way into the press, most often left-wing or centre-left publications (*Le Monde, Libération, Le Nouvel Observateur, l'Humanité*), but sometimes also television and radio when the verdict is particularly severe. At the other end of the political spectrum, the government and the majority sometimes receive the opposite criticism—that their penal policy is not harsh enough—from victim associations categorized as right-wing (such as the *Institute for Justice*, founded by the father of a murdered woman), police unions (such as *Synergie*) and the most conservative fringes of the aforementioned majority (for example those making up the collective called *The Popular Right*).

These diverse actors present an opportunity to consider the connections between the different forms of knowledge produced on prisons. In his work on the links that

---

7   *Commission nationale consultative des droits de l'homme.*

8   The inspector's reports are available online: http://www.cglpl.fr/ref.

9   Created following the scandal of the 2000s, this commission was, despite its protests, absorbed by a new authority, the Human Rights Ombudsman (*le Défenseur des droits*).

10   In 2011 it was, like other rights protection authorities and in spite of protests, absorbed by a new institution, the "Defender of Rights" ("*Défenseur des droits*").

exist between expert and nonexpert knowledge, Pierre Lascoumes constructed a typology based on two criteria: how the public issue is constructed (from the top down or vice versa), and the nature of the knowledge brought into play (either institutional or based on personal experience). Combining these criteria brings four types into relief. A cause constructed "from the top", based on institutional knowledge, represents the classic form of official expertise. A cause based on activism "from the bottom"—based on feedback from actors—is the common model of political problem construction by people and groups whose voices are left out of traditional expertise. The intermediate models are interesting because they reflect links that are less often mentioned: an assessment "from the bottom" can bring institutional knowledge into play if it is implemented by critical professionals. For example, in the early 1970s, the GISTI Immigrant Information and Support Group, an organisation fighting for the rights of foreign nationals, was created by young senior government officials mobilizing their legal expertise (Israël 2009). Similarly, criticism based on experience can be structured according to a "from-the-top" model, if the organized activists pool their experiences and broadcast them. Pierre Lascoumes explains that this typology is valuable not so much because it provides a rigid framework, but because it makes it easier to examine "moves (circulation and alliance) from one type of epistemology to another, as well as the ways in which rationalities are combined during the mobilization process" (Lascoumes 2011). In fact, "arguments often circulate from one space to another with the different recoding that accompanies them", and "this is all the more so because it has become compulsory for demands to pass through the media before being recognized".

We do not intend to classify the "prison cause" as one specific type, but rather to see which features it borrows from each of them. Historically, the structure of the Correctional Service has been based on a very hierarchical model resistant to nonexpert criticism. The CS tables reforms that it deems necessary based on its own expertise. And yet, the reform that came under discussion at the turn of the 20th century was partly a response to calls "from the bottom", and the CS was faced with the need to change according to watchwords not of its own choosing. On the other hand, the movements of the 1970s, which inspire current critical expression, centered their demands on the right to speak. They wanted opinions based on experience to enter the public arena. The struggle for this right to speak "from the bottom" sometimes proceeded spectacularly (in the form of a riot for example), but more often quietly. These critical words were relayed by permanent activist structures that embodied the experience-based discourse model, but the discourse is pooled and then presented in the same format as expert criticism, by groups such as IPW[11]. Finally, institutions that exist for the purpose of consultation rather than decision-making produce critical discourse that is addressed just as much "to the top"—to bring about change in the Correctional Service—as "to the bottom", supporting and legitimizing activist discourse.

Our aim is to describe this interweaving. However, the plurality of levels of expression should not obscure the fact that these diverse elaborations are also concurrent. And they become even more concurrent as the real reform approaches, when it becomes necessary move beyond coexisting propositions and choose those which the CS and government consider possible or desirable. We want to show both the juxtaposition of voices *and* their unequal power relationship. The story this books tells is largely that of how the Correctional Service went about recovering its position of expertise after the proliferation of critical authorities and critical discourse. In spite of this recovery, unresolved points of conflict still exist and are shifting, for example, from activist groups to official authorities and opposition parties. And it obviously does not put an end to prisoners' critical abilities.

---

11   These two dimensions are, more broadly, inseparable from the professionalisation trend within these types of associations, in which distinctions are made between activists who have been around since the very beginning and young professionals recruited "outside" the traditional activist field. On a similar trend in the feminist field, see (Flahault and Loiseau 2008).

This objective is linked to our respective research, and will be based on various studies we conducted over a period of ten years. We will briefly describe this research.

Historian Jean Bérard's work on prison issues began with a study of the history of prison-related activism in the 1970s (Bérard 2010). In the context of his thesis, he extended this study to the relationships between the justice system and the various movements that arose after May 1968 (revolutionary, feminist, homosexual, anti-racist) (Bérard 2013). While working for the French section of IPW, he linked these questions to the contemporary practices of prisoner rights activists. In this context, he contributed to a report on prison conditions (OIP, 2005), based on cross-linked official data, prisoner interviews and studies conducted by the association. He also contributed to a CNCDH study on alternatives to incarceration (CNCDH, 2007b). In collaboration with a jurist, he worked on appeals lodged in French courts by long-sentence prisoners, to expose their prison conditions (de Suremain and Bérard 2009). He also helped coordinate an unprecedented survey of French prisoners' reform expectations, organized by a group of associations and unions. In particular, he designed a questionnaire that was completed by over 15,000 prisoners, and then he helped analyze the results and turn them into reform proposals. Finally, through observations and interviews, he studied a charitable project that aided released prisoners who had no resources or plans (Bérard 2011). In these different contexts, he worked on documentary sources of the 1970s, public debates at the turn of the 21st century, reform projects, and conducted interviews with actors in legal and prison systems.

Sociologist Gilles Chantraine's work focuses on the contemporary transformation of prisons (mainly in France but also in Europe, see Chantraine et al., 2007), a subject that lies at the junction between the sociology of total institutions, the sociology of individual prison experiences and the sociology of professions. In *Par-delà les murs* (Chantraine, 2004), building on the work of Erving Goffman, he tested the concept of the total institution, measuring it against the diverse relationships that exist between incarceration and the social and personal history of prisoners. The methodological apparatus—based on life stories told by people confined in jails—enabled data on the *ordinary, banal, everyday* lives of prisoners to emerge. Contrary to a certain type of reassuring, purely utilitarian criminology (Carrier, Chantraine, 2009) that focuses on the criminal and his "personality", flaws, "pathologies", "dangerousness" and chances of "redemption", he instead analyzed the social, structural and longitudinal processes that link the lives of individuals to the penal system and prison.

Next, Gilles Chantraine conducted research into three so-called "medium-security" Canadian penitentiaries, on the basis of semi-structured interviews and ethnographical observations. The study, which explored new forms of behaviour control in detention, focused particularly on the role of formal leaders (members of prisoner committees) in the production of order in prison (Chantraine 2006), on the professional practices of psycho-social experts in prison, and on how the power they wield over prisoners generates infrapolitical resistance that is part of the fabric of everyday prison life. Finally, from 2009 to 2011, he was the director of a collective research project on prisons for minors (Chantraine, dir, 2011), that aimed to understand individual incarceration experiences (with the problems and adaptations these entail), the practices of professionals (their routines and the clashes between them), and public controversies (with their peaks and slack periods). To this end, several methods were combined: prison ethnography, interviews with professionals and young prisoners, and two sets of group interviews with various professionals working in the prison (guards, tutors, healthcare professionals and teaching personnel). In parallel with these different field studies, Gilles Chantraine conducted theoretical and/or transversal examinations of the current state of research in prisons (2000; 2004), on the history of prison's social functions (Chantraine 2010), on the use of law in prison (Chantraine and Kaminski, 2007; Salle and Chantraine, 2009), on suicide prevention practices in prison (Cliquennois and Chantraine,

2009); and on the sociology of risk in the penal and penitentiary fields (Cauchie and Chantraine, 2005; Chantraine and Cauchie, 2006; Bérard and Chantraine, 2011).

Let it be said from the outset: this book does not reconstruct a particular study, nor synthesize these different works. Instead it uses these various studies to address a specific problem: how do the voices of various actors within the prison system combine and compete? We wanted to examine these materials by analyzing how they interplay, in a sequence organized around a reform process. Attempting to interweave these different voices entails certain risks.

The first risk lies in the use of heterogeneous materials, which were originally produced for more targeted studies, and could thus lose the methodological coherence of the initial data set. In particular, our goal is neither to exhaustively describe individuals' diverse relationships to incarceration, nor to understand all of the sociological characteristics of incarcerated persons. By choosing to work on how prisoners express political conflict, collecting data in a variety of contexts, we accept that there is a certain bias inherent in relaying opinions that are no doubt held only by a minority. We do not claim that these represent what everyone is thinking. We try to demonstrate that these shed a counterbalancing light on the dominant political and institutional opinion. The second risk lies in describing the history of a present moment with all of the limitations this entails: a lack of distance, a lack of internal sources from the Correctional Service, and the difficulty of defining the scope of available sources. Therefore, there is an element of experimentation in this work, not an attempt at a literary genre but more simply an endeavour that is conscious of its obvious limits.

We do not believe that these limits compromise the specific contribution of our approach. In fact, a considerable number of books examine prison reform (for example Foucault 1977; Ignatieff 1978; Mathiesen 2006), from the punitive turn to the social functions of prison (for example Jacobsen 2005; Tonry 1995; Tonry 2001; Gottschalk 2006), and everyday prison life (for example Irwin 2001; Irwin

2009; Crewe 2009). But in France, these levels of analysis are rarely joined together, making it difficult to grasp the consequences that penal policies have within prisons (on social relationships in custody). In this sense, we wish to carry on the tradition of sociological research on contemporary prison policies (for example Marc Mauer and the Sentencing Project 2006; Barker 2009; Garland 2002; Wacquant 2009), while attempting, following the example of the Anglophone research tradition, represented by the *Journal of Prisoners on Prison* (Gaucher 1988, Gaucher 2002), and that of *convict criminology* (Ross and Richards 2003), of rooting this criticism in prisoners' concrete experience. The book aims to draw attention to the kinds of barriers and connections that exist between opinions expressed behind prison doors and the debate's public manifestations. By overlapping different levels of observation—from prisoners' stories to parliamentary debates—we endeavour to examine how infrapolitical forms of resistance are transferred, received, translated and transformed into legitimate forms of political discussion, as well as the government's responses to these interpellations. To put it simply, we want to revive the tradition of breaking the silence to which the penal system condemns its subjects.

This book is designed to effect a kind of *gradation* as it reconstructs the taking of positions; it begins by observing how the government conceived its reform, gradually introduces the actors involved in its criticism, and then advances to the perspective of the prisoners themselves. The first chapters tell of the conception and implementation of the penitentiary law, by reconstructing the sequence of penal changes that, in part, brought it into being.

To begin with, we will show that the Correctional Service's first challenge was to control the conception of the text and impose a monopoly of legitimate, professional knowledge (chapter 1). Its thinking was formulated along two major axes. The first consisted of linking the question of rights to an increase in the number of prisons—in other words making "modernization" the principal means of "humanizing" prison conditions (chapter 2). The second axis aimed to base the legitimacy of the new planned management approach (the legal creation of differential detention regimes) on the evaluation and control of risks generated by the detention of persons considered more or less dangerous. To counter this central point of the reform, left-wing MPs drew attention to the fact that it contradicted the ostensible objective of defining and protecting the rights of all detained persons. Although these political conflicts did not jeopardize the final passing of the law, they nevertheless signalled the failure of the right-wing majority's attempt to secure a political consensus (chapter 3). Furthermore, the Correctional Service sought new ways of managing the flow of prison admissions, particularly by making increased use of electronic bracelets. Thus we will be examining the tensions between the different scenes of penal policy: between, on the one hand, the political arena with its proclamations about the need to punish offenders more severely, and, on the other hand, the professional and administrative arena where administrative solutions are sought, particularly with the goal of reducing carceral overpopulation (chapter 4). The tension between these different arenas, discourses and endeavours increases when highly publicized recidivism cases become emotional fulcrums for those in power. Consequently, the "necessity" of evaluating prisoners' recidivism risk is coupled with the injunction to prevent the release of prisoners who are considered dangerous. What these two complementary objectives have in common is that they are based on a political desire to share knowledge and skills between judges, penal administration representatives and the medical profession. We will examine the effect these endeavours have on prisoner treatment and, more broadly, on the definition of prisoners' rights (chapter 5).

As a counterpoint, we will next (chapter 6) examine the case of a group of prisoners serving very long sentences who collectively denounced their fate by provocatively and ironically requesting that the death penalty be applied to themselves if they were going to be left without any hope of release. We will show that this kind of transgressive act (a prohibited petition) is the obverse of the institution's efforts to silence prisoners, and that in this respect, this sort of act—no doubt more than any other—exposes the contradictions between professing respect for rights, lengthening sentences, and focusing prison policy on security. Then we will examine the prison question from the perspective of repeat offenders: their social trajectories, criminal careers and incarceration experiences (chapter 7). We will show that incorporating the "ineluctability" of prison—a "hard fate" as defined by Bourdieu (1999)—for "habitual offenders" refutes all hopes for corrective prisons and leads, on the contrary, to the development of nonexpert knowledge on incarceration, as well as infrapolitics that expose a system of police, courts and prisons that caters to the dominant classes. We will base an extension of this analysis on a focused study of the experiences of released prisoners (chapter 8). We will explore how the experiential and infrapolitical knowledge of the people who pass through the justice system can shift the debate (or should shift it, if only the authorities were willing to acknowledge the need). It is no longer simply a matter of questioning whether or not prisons have the ability to correct deviant behaviour, or of denouncing intolerable material living conditions. It is more broadly a matter of revealing what was not visible in the political debates analyzed in the first part of this book, showing how the carceral system constitutes one cog in the machinery used to discipline the poor, how prison mechanisms function, and how these mechanisms are *also* reproduced outside prison.

CHAPTER 1
Conceiving the reform

A legislative discussion on the prison system, that political "bad object" (Artières, Lascoumes and Salle 2004), is a rare event. A penitentiary law was indeed passed in 1987. But it comprised only six articles, and its essential purpose was to set out a new redistribution of responsibilities between the public and private sectors[12]. The most recent significant reforms were essentially carried out through decrees and circulars (Bérard 2010). One reason for this is that the period that began with the opposition movements of the 1970s marked "the end of utopias" in matters relating to prisons (Faugeron 2002). To understand why, it is necessary to briefly review the history of prison reform discourse.

Typology and chronology of reform discourse

According to Claude Faugeron and Jean-Michel Boulaire, the first category of prison discourse "finds its rationality in a theory of punishment" (Faugeron and Le Boulaire 1991). It can be divided into two types. The first is "represented by a positive representation of human nature". It "attributes to prison sentences a social value, that of individual change". In 19th-century France, the best-known harbinger of this school of thought was philanthropic lawyer and correctional theoretician Charles Lucas. The second rationale is characterized by a pessimistic representation of mankind.

---

12   The law of 22 June 1987 relating to the penitentiary public service.

It attributes to punishment "traditional functions of deterrence, intimidation and neutralization". The most famous proponent of this approach was Alexis de Tocqueville who, upon his return from the United States, fought against the ineffective generosity of the philanthropists (Petit 1998).

In the prison debate, lines of opposition are repeatedly drawn between prisons that correct and prisons that intimidate. And yet, in Faugeron and Le Boulaire's view, these two rationales ultimately serve the same purpose: the legitimization of prison (Faugeron and Le Boulaire 1991). Both justify the idea of striving for good prisons that are effective at reducing crime and fighting recidivism, which is a real thorn in the side of penal systems. Their shared foundation is prison science, over which proponents of the two approaches battle for dominance. As Jean-Jacques Petit explains, "prison science has a very ambitious task: to resolve the issue of criminality, to eliminate or at least limit recidivism through an appropriate imprisonment regime" (Petit 1998).

By contrast, another category of discourse is characterized as "pragmatic", because it concerns prison conditions and can do without a theory of punishment. Within this category, Faugeron and Le Boulaire distinguish two different types. The first is said to be "critical", denouncing "on the one hand, dilapidated buildings, prison overcrowding, insufficient hygiene—in short, the inhumanity of the structure; on the other hand, the contagion of immorality, the sharing of criminal methods—in short, the inability to prevent crime". The second variety is the so-called "expert" discourse of prison "practitioners" (Faugeron and Le Boulaire 1991). This encompasses the discourse of the Correctional Service, but also includes that of doctors, teachers, psychologists, social workers and tutors.

These categories of discourse are not impervious to one another, and many combinations can be imagined. For example, first-time offenders might be subject to a "rehabilitation" regime. Hardened repeat offenders might be subjected to the "necessary severity" that will finally put them on the straight and narrow path to which educational efforts failed to direct them. The reverse is also possible. Those handed short sentences could experience a harsh, deterrent prison term to ensure that their first incarceration is their last. Those handed long sentences could benefit from efforts to enable eventual rehabilitation. All of these different types of discourse have one thing in common: when prison is called into question as an institution, they posit reform as the solution to its failure. How can it be that this always appears to be the fruit of a new, clear-sighted reconsideration of the incarceration issue? This is because (and this is the second point we borrow from Claude Faugeron and Jean-Michel Le Boulaire) since the early 19th century, prison reform discourse has passed through cycles of activation, criticism, oblivion and return (Faugeron and Le Boulaire 1991).

The first phase of critical discourse gave pride of place to correctional theoreticians. This was the time of the *Société royale des prisons* (the Royal Society of Prisons) under the Bourbon Restoration (1815-1830), and of the pre-eminence of Charles Lucas. This discourse was subject to increasingly aggressive challenges during the first decade of the July Monarchy (1830-1848). A discourse favouring deterrence arose in opposition to the philanthropic discourse, which was accused to generating recidivism. But over the years that followed, the results remained unfavourable to proponents of both schools of thought, and all hope in prison science dried up. The advent of the criminal record and the perfecting of criminal statistics under the Second French Empire (1852-1870) meant that, as Bernard Schnapper noted, "almost every year, ministers made alarmed comments" on the recidivism issue (Schnapper 1983). This is why the great parliamentary inquiry on the prison system in 1872 marked the end of the 19th century prison reform debate. The exhaustion of reformist discourse opened the door to the introduction, after 1870, of suspended sentences and parole, as well as the policy of carceral population reduction that was pursued until the interwar period. These advances were, however, counterbalanced by a lack of concern for prisons and prisoner wellbeing (Badinter 1992).

Prison reform discourse resumed after the liberation of France. Paul Amor, a magistrate and resistance fighter imprisoned during the Occupation, became the director of the Correctional Service and launched a reform that borrowed a number of precepts from the philanthropic school: differential regimes according to status (defendant or prisoner) and, in the case of convicted criminals, according to "gender, personality and the extent of the criminal's corruption"; the obligation to work; the promotion of teaching, training, social services, medical and psychological services, and prison personnel training. But these reforms were applied unevenly and were opposed by proponents of increased severity. The issue of prison security came to the fore at the outbreak of the Algerian War. The incarceration of FLN and OAS militants, and their occasional escapes, caused leading French authorities to take a more hard-line stance. After the revolts of the 1970s, debates no longer centred on prison theories, but focused instead the harshness of prison conditions and the arbitrariness of Correctional Service decisions. The years 1971-1974 were marked by a serious crisis in the prison system. Its most visible manifestations were acts of violence between prisoners and prison staff amid revolts and escape attempts, some of which succeeded, though others were quashed with extreme brutality. In July 1971, a prisoner in Lyon fatally wounded a guard. In September, two prisoners in Clairvaux—Claude Buffet and Roger Bontems—attempted to escape by taking a nurse and guard hostage; they executed them when the police stormed in. In reprisal, the Minister of Justice banned Christmas parcels, and this sparked several protests. The largest was the revolt at the Toul prison. In January 1972, the rebellion reached the Nancy prison, and in February there were further protests at prisons in Amiens, Lille and Nîmes. In June, the Nancy rebels were convicted. In January 1973, a strike took place at the Melun detention centre. In April, prisoners in Lyon staged a hunger strike. In May, they climbed onto the roof and damaged their cells. In September, a revolt erupted at La Santé jail, with prisoners climbing onto the roof. In February 1974, a young prisoner named Patrick Mirval died in Fleury-Mérogis, and evidence suggested he had been beaten. In June, another revolt at La Santé: a prisoner staged a hunger strike, demanding to be allowed access to the books of his choice. In July, several prisons were in turmoil. Several revolts broke out, and as they were quelled several people died. The summer of 1974 marked the culmination of the protest.

A short time before these revolts, new activist groups arose outside of the prison walls. In February 1971, Michel Foucault, Jean-Marie Domenach and Pierre Vidal-Naquet founded the Prison Information Group (GIP)[13] (Artières, Quéro and Zancarini-Fournel 2003; Salle 2004). In May and June, the group published its first pamphlets. In June 1972, on the initiative of a young doctor by the name of Antoine Lazarus, the Prisons Multiprofessional Group (GMP)[14] was founded, with the aim of enabling everyone involved with prisons to get together and exchange information and ideas. In June, the GIP was dissolved, giving way to the Prisoners' Action Committee (CAP)[15] and the Association for the Defence of Prisoners' Rights (ADDD)[16].

The reforms undertaken in 1972 and 1975 attempted to improve living conditions without relying on a new theory of punishment, stressing the need to limit recourse to incarceration.

Thus the prison issue went through a correction-deterrence-scepticism cycle similar to that of a century earlier, but this time condensed into a shorter period. The reforms initiated in the 1970s did not have time to generate divisions between first-rate orators who were also penal system theorists. The issue of public security has taken the place

---

13   *"Groupe d'information sur les prisons".*
14   *"Groupe multiprofessionnel des prisons".*
15   *"Comité d'action des prisonniers".*
16   *"l'Association pour la défense des droits des détenus".*

of prison issues, relegating prison questions to a secondary status (Bonelli 2007a; Bonelli 2007b). The reforms of the 1970s differ from those of the 19th century in that, whereas the Third French Republic counterbalanced the end of high hopes for prison reform with restrictions on its use, since the 1970s, dwindling faith in the virtues of incarceration has been accompanied by a steady increase in the prison population. The prison influx is fuelled by dynamics outside of prisons, and there no longer exists any theoretical model justifying their use. In other words, the CS's primary responsibility is to manage an institution that is being used more and more at a time when people have given up expecting it to turn into what it was always supposed to be but has never become.

The scandal of arbitrariness and the management of rising carceral populations

The string of events that resulted in the passing of the 2009 penitentiary law reflected this paradox. As pointed out in the introduction, it began in 2000 with a public scandal that ensued following the exposure of the dilapidated and decayed state of French prisons, leading to a legislative undertaking being placed the policy agenda (Salle 2009). Its objective was twofold. First, it aimed to rectify the "arbitrariness" of prisons, in other words to remedy the state of prison law, which was essentially composed of infra-legislative texts, a situation that was derided through the widespread use of the expressions "sub-law" and "non-law" to characterize penitentiary law. Next, loopholes in the monitoring of the application of these texts needed to be closed. A reform was drawn up by the left-wing government in power between 1997 and 2002, but it was abandoned in the final months of the legislature, at a time when public safety once again became a central issue. Facing accusations of being weak in the fight against crime, Socialist Prime Minister Lionel Jospin did not want to pass a law regarded as "favourable to offenders".

However, 2000-2005 was a period when the state of French 35 prisons was being repeatedly denounced by activists and academics (OIP 2005), and it was also a time of significant institutional production on the guiding lines of a penitentiary reform, by MPs (Mermaz and Floch 2000; Hyest and Cabanel 2000), by a commission presided by a senior judge (Canivet 2000), by the National Consultative Commission on Human Rights (CNCDH 2007a), and, at another level, by the Council of Europe (Council of Europe 2009). In accordance with their different methodologies, these actors considered ways to "bring the constitutional state into prison", in other words to recognize, codify and guarantee prisoners' rights while monitoring the CS's exercise of power. A report by senior judge Guy Canivet recommended the development of a corpus of "quality standards that are accessible, precise and predictable". He stressed that "the infeasibility of the rules and the excessive amount of interpretation they leave to the Correctional Service are the source of disputes and frustration". According to him:

> "...this latitude, apparently beneficial to prison personnel, in fact harms them through the constant indecision in which it places them, as well as through the tolerance it authorizes. In the long run, the unequal treatment it engenders can only provoke a disorder prejudicial to the personnel themselves. Standards and their application must be consistent and equal for all, and should not be varied according to the prisoner, the guard or the establishment".

These reformative programs constituted new policy developments in the area of prisons. The aim was no longer "foundational" (Faugeron and Le Boulaire 1992), basing the legitimation of incarceration on a belief in its therapeutic and/or redemptive virtues[17]. Now it essentially concerned

---

17   In this sense, theories of rehabilitation through prison share more similarities than differences with theories of retribution and deterrence. Three central elements underpinning both are: 1) the obligation to punish, 2) punishment as a source of suffering, and 3) prison as the standard punishment (Garcia 2009).

conceptions of the defence of individuals *against the institution*. The CNCDH provided a general formulation of this movement towards formalizing rights protection:

> "The CNCDH recommends that a hierarchy of priorities be respected in the definition of the legal status of persons deprived of freedom.
>
> An incarcerated person is, and remains, in the full sense, a "human person" whose fundamental rights cannot be ignored. Consequently, the state is subject to various obligations to guarantee, under all circumstances, respect for individual liberty.
>
> On a second level, an incarcerated person remains a "citizen". This characteristic feature of domestic law serves as a reminder that the grounds for incarceration can in no case justify a separation from the rest of society. Prison should no longer be only conceived as an eviction.
>
> On a third level, an incarcerated person remains a "person subject to trial" benefitting from procedural rights (the adversarial principle, the right of judicial remedy) normally provided for in the matters under consideration. Prison law, in effect, deals with questions of a mixed legal nature that simultaneously concern administrative law, penal law, civic law and labour law. The guarantees established in these disciplines must be applied to prisoners.
>
> On a fourth level, an incarcerated person must be regarded as a "user" having a relationship—compulsory of course—with an administrative public service. As a result, prisoners can benefit from the right to a normal functioning of the service in relation to themselves and in the implementation of the tasks assigned to public power by the law" (CNCDH 2007a).

What is interesting about this proposal is that it takes seriously the idea that an incarcerated person is only deprived of the freedom to come and go, and disregards the consequences of this conception. It expresses an obvious logical fact (by what right would prisoners be deprived of other rights?) that also represents a complete break with everything that underpins the disciplinary organization of prison. These formulations furnish a reformist perspective that could enable concrete steps to be taken towards protecting prisoners and recognizing rights. But they also constitute a permanent critical authority. The idea of prisons functioning fully in accordance with these orientations is utopian. It is not utopian in the spirit of the 19th century reformists, who dreamed of a prison structure perfectly tailored to the transformation of criminals. But it is indeed utopian in the sense that a prison capable of completely respecting rights would be completely different from contemporary prisons, in terms of its material organization as well as its operating guidelines. Therefore, these recommendations operate both as triggers of legal change, and as ideal standards for comparing the concrete situation of prisoners to their due rights as a whole.

And yet, these reflections found no political relay, because the 2000-2005 period was marked by a reverse policy trend, characterized by a disjunction between the imperative to draft legislation protective of rights and the penitentiary policy actually pursued, centred around expanding security measures and increasing the number of prisons. This disjunction put an end to the political consensus stemming from the 2000 scandal and enabled the Correctional Service to develop another reform rationale.

This new rationale began by breaking with a central idea behind pro-rights recommendations: raising the development of penitentiary law to the legislative level. Beginning in 2002, right-wing justice ministers concentrated their policy efforts on penal law in the belief that, without political damage, they could leave it up to the Correctional Service to make the necessary changes to the prison system. Their policy of penal severity produced renewed, rapid carceral population growth: there were 49,718 prisoners on 1 July 2001, 60,963 on 1 July 2003, 62,438 on 1 July 2005 and 64,616 on 1 July 2007 (Aubusson de Cavarlay 2008).

This trend alone exacerbated tensions in prisons, leading the Correctional Service to demand reinforced means of maintaining order (Chauvenet, Rostaing and Orlic 2008).

A number of changes were made to boost prison security, following guidelines provided by Minister of Justice Dominique Perben (UMP party)[18]: the creation of a department of security within the Correctional Service Administration, the implementation of regional response and security teams (ERIS) modelled after police response teams, the installation or consolidation of anti-helicopter ropes, the introduction of extensive technology such as cell phone scrambling systems, biometrics and X-ray tunnels, the improvement of perimeter security posts, the installation of glacis around prisons, the reduction of movement within prisons—for example by keeping cell doors closed in the central buildings. In 2003 alone, some thirty notes or circulars relating to security were drafted.

During these years there was a strong tendency to experiment with changes to the operation of certain detention regimes. Outside of all legal reform, the CS implemented differential regimes. It imposed a "doors closed" regime in certain wings of detention centres (correctional facilities more oriented towards rehabilitation than prisons, which focus on security) where prisoners were previously allowed to circulate during part of the daytime (Cliquennois 2009). At the very moment when reports were piling up explaining the need for legislation ending a "regime of lawlessness", the minister, without any new legal foundation, was experimenting with a new system of differential prisoner rights management.

Mastering reform

This was how all prisons bills ended up being shelved between 2002 and 2007. But in 2007, Nicolas Sarkozy, then on the presidential campaign trail, made a commitment to pass a penitentiary law, making it inevitable that a legislative text would be introduced. This new undertaking inherited

---

18   "I not only want to make escapes virtually impossible, but above all I want to reinforce staff security because I'm thinking primarily of them" (in Bérard and Coye 2005)

characteristics from the two contradictory lines of reformist thought that had been developing since 2000: on the one hand the promotion of rights a the public legitimation of reform, on the other hand the pursuit of changes to detention management as an administrative objective. A central challenge for the Correctional Service was to get lawmakers to validate these new orientations.

The law creation process embodied both of these dimensions. In August 2007, Justice Minister Rachida Dati established a "Restricted Steering Committee" (RSC) that was required to submit a summary of its work in October 2007 "to accompany the legislative bill's introduction in Parliament and enlighten the future work of deputies and senators" (COR 2007). She defined the law's ambition thus: "We must guarantee the fundamental rights of detained persons while providing concrete answers to the questions raised by the implementation of these rights".

But at the same time, the passing of a law that imposed strict minimum prison sentences for repeat offenders led the Correctional Service to prepare for continued carceral population growth, and define its own conception of reform issues in an internal chancellery document, distributed to the RSC and then leaked to activists. According to the Correctional Service Administration, these various changes would result in "a significant increase in the [prison] population, which could reach 80,000 by 2017". Likely trends were enumerated: more "elderly" prisoners and young prisoners aged 18 to 35; longer long-term sentences and a sharp increase in short sentences; finally the CS believed the presence of prisoners of Eastern European origin would increase violence in prisons (Direction de l'administration pénitentiaire 2007).

The Correctional Service Administration rightly pointed out that it had no power to make decisions regarding carceral admission inflows and sentence adjustments. On this basis it concluded that the various development angles it was proposing did not depend on the administration itself but on "judges taking prison overpopulation into account when making sentence adjustment decisions"[19]. The CS regarded this as a pragmatic approach that should be supported by a just-in-time flow policy characterized by "optimal use of existing prisons": "controlling overpopulation", "renewed relations with inter-regional directors", etc. These concerns of the CS also explain why the minister and the CS were both proclaiming the objective of developing sentence adjustments.

Why was it necessary to lock up greater numbers of people? The CS kept silent on this point, except to say that France was not Europe's worst student when it came to imprisonment rates. The document only compared France to countries with higher rates (Spain, England and Holland, whose 2004 rates were, respectively: 142.4, 142.7 and 133.9 prisoners per 100,000 residents, as compared to 76.4 in Denmark and 78.3 in Sweden). There was no mention of Finland, which had succeeded in significantly reducing its imprisonment rate by trying to adopt the Scandinavian models (Brodeur 2006). In 2004, Finland had 73 prisoners for every 100,000 residents as compared to 91.8 in France.

At the same time, the Correctional Service Administration launched a concerted attack against all challenges to existing penal policy, reducing these to an "abolitionist trend, [...] fuelled by the writings of Michel Foucault," which made prisons "a subject of ideology" (Direction de l'administration pénitentiaire 2007). "Abolitionism" came to be the spectre that the Correctional Service's senior management invoked against all radical criticism of their policy orientations[20]. Far from these "ideological" discussions, the administration's forecasted ten-year, 20,000-prisoner increase was not discussed at all. For example, Rachida Dati asked the RSC to examine the prison conditions of "people suffering from deteriorating

---

19   *Ibid.*

20   See for example the grandstanding of Jean-Marie Bockel, then Secretary of State for Justice, "Let us not exclude prison from the arena of democratic deliberation", *Le Monde*, 13 October 2009: "Certain emblematic figures of anti-prison activism hardly burden themselves with methodological scruples to better track down, behind every hint of discomfort in prison, the justification of the abolishment of prisons".

mental faculties" and "the elderly, who are the most often socially excluded", without addressing the problem of their very presence in prison. In its view, merely raising the question of possibly handling them in a non-penitentiary context probably stemmed from the "ideology" of the "abolitionist currents". The CS completed the disconnect between, on the one hand, the objectives and discourse of penal policy (reducing crime, preventing recidivism) and, on the other hand, the limits to managing the consequences of this policy. It strongly pitted its administrative reasoning against any political challenge to the use of incarceration: "French prisons are not shameful", "France manages its prisons well" (Direction de l'administration pénitentiaire 2007). The anticipation of carceral population growth, of the likely persistence of overcrowding, and—according to the CSA—of an "increase in the duration of long sentences" and of a "sharp increase in instances of violence in prison, suffered by prisoners and staff alike", cast a dark shadow over hopes of any real change in the situation.

Optional rights

In 2007, the Correctional Service made an important symbolic gesture by announcing that it would be implementing the European Prison Rules (EPR), a new version of which had been passed in January 2006. These rules were first drawn up in 1973 by the Council of Europe. At the time, it was a matter of Europe minimally adopting all of the United Nation's rules for the treatment of prisoners, drafted in 1955. The EPR were revised in 1987, and again in 2006, to incorporate Council of Europe recommendations as well as the advances of the European Court of Human Rights. The Correctional Service's subscription to these non-binding recommendations is therefore significant. But this move towards a *rights policy* was deeply ambivalent. Following the minister's example, the Correctional Service Administration did indeed set itself the objective of applying the European Prison Rules[21], and in 2007 claimed to be experimenting with eight of them (out of 108) in 28 establishments (out of 190)[22]. The favour shown to the EPR had two meanings. On the one hand there was formal acceptance of the recognition of prisoners' rights. On the other hand there was the repeated emphasis on the "non-binding", "non-mandatory" character of the rules, "most of which should be applied to the extent possible". It does not take much to claim that rules applied "to the extent possible" are being respected. If they are not being applied, one must simply assume that it would be impossible to do so! Especially since the Correctional Service implemented them through experimentation with pilot sites, not through a system-wide rollout of new rights. By contrast, it was not a question of applying precise recommendations specific to French penitentiary law like those of the March 2004 *Study on Human Rights in Prison* by the National Consultative Commission on Human Rights (CNCDH 2007a).

From this perspective, the European Prison Rules (EPR) established by the Council of Europe provide ambiguous guidance. They are based on the two-pronged approach of recognizing rights and distinguishing detention regimes according to a "risk" evaluation. The first element is central, and represents the core principles affirmed by the rules. But they also stipulate that all prisoners should be evaluated "to determine the risk that they would present to the community in case of escape, (and) the probability that they would attempt to escape either alone or with the help of outside accomplices" (Council of Europe 2009). Consequently, every prisoner must submit "to a security regime corresponding to the level of risk identified", the necessary level

---

21   Council of Europe, *Recommendation on the European Prison Rules*, 2006, in Council of Europe (2009).
22   Such as the separation of defendants and convicts in jails, the formalization of the procedure for receiving prisoners in an establishment, the implementation of a formalized procedure for handling prisoners' requests. Circular of the Correctional Service Administration of 14 January 2009 relating to the gradual introduction of the EPR in penitentiary establishments according to five priorities defined for their ability to help the prison system develop.

being "regularly reevaluated"[23]. It is worth mentioning that this provision in the EPR is not so much intended to legitimize this form of classification... as to prevent its abuse. As jurist Martine Herzog-Evans writes: "Indeed, rule 51.4 lays down the principle that all prisoners must submit to a security regime that corresponds to their identified risk level. The comments made about this by the Council of Europe specify that when this question was addressed on the occasion of the 2006 revision of the EPR, it was because of member states' increasing use of differential regimes" (Herzog-Evans 2010). Nevertheless, those who promoted differential detention regimes invoked this rule to legitimize their reform efforts.

The Restricted Steering Committee relied on the EPR to formulate its reform recommendations. But its report was immediately contested, particularly by the French section of International Prison Watch[24], because it did not contain the general objective of legislatively transposing the recommendations of French human rights bodies. The association pointed out that the committee's report, ostensibly intended to define a set of constructive new proposals, in fact played a game of double-edged tactical effectiveness. On the one hand, by producing a new report, it was effectively distancing itself from previous texts dealing with the formalization of prisoners' rights, texts that were more specific and potentially restrictive for the CS. On the other hand, it ensured that the CS's priorities were integrated into the report itself. For example, some "recommendations reveal themselves to be the exact—or nearly exact— reproduction of the Correctional Service Administration's own expectations, which were communicated to the RSC in the form of "hypotheses" as it carried out its work"[25]. This was the case in the matter of disciplinary cell punishment duration, which the RSC wished to see set at 28 days, more or less corresponding

---

23   Council of Europe, *Recommendation on the European Prison Rules*, 2006, in Council of Europe (2009).

24   International Prison Watch - French section, press release 21/10/07, "*Comité d'orientation restreint sur la loi pénitentiaire: un rapport ni fait ni à faire*".

25   *Ibid.*

to the intentions of the chancellery (30 days), even though this duration is, for example, three times that allowed by the 2001 Belgian law (9 days). The Minister of Justice did not have much trouble boasting that a significant number of the RSC's recommendations would be represented in a legislative bill that the CS had drafted from cover to cover.

Thus, over time, the justice ministry absorbed not only the shock of the scandal that had begun in 2000, but also the subversive dimension of the many reports and reform recommendations written in its aftermath. This strategy took two forms. First, the adoption of the reference to the European Prison Rules. Next, the claim that these rules were "only" recommendations from which the government could pick and choose as it pleased. The establishment of a final working group (the RSC) that was required to formulate proposals in a limited time helped shield the minister's legislative bill from the most ambitious recommendations. The way in which the bill itself appeared in the press is significant. On 10 June 2007, the text of the bill was disclosed through an opportune leak to the tabloid newspaper *Le Parisien,* in the context of a central theme: the struggle against overcrowding through the increased use of sentence adjustments and alternatives to prison.[26] This first communication operation concerning such a highly anticipated bill was surprising for two reasons. First, because it announced Rachida Dati's plan to empty prisons, only a year after the promulgation of the minimum sentences law—which was essentially Rachida Dati's execution of Nicolas Sarkozy's plan to fill up prisons. Second, because it remained relatively silent about the reform's original objective. According to the formulas that had been constantly repeated over a period of ten years, the law was supposed to be primarily about putting an end to prison's legal exception, giving prisoners a legal status, and enshrining the application of ordinary law behind the walls.

This stunt enabled the central objective of the reform to be shifted, away from concern for protecting prisoners against

---

26   "Le Plan Dati pour vider les prisons", *Le Parisien,* 10 June 2008.

the risk of arbitrariness, towards the legitimation of new forms of management and administration. This was made possible by discrediting radical prison criticism, professing partial reformist objectives, concentrating the effort on increasing the number of custodial institutions and promoting risk management. From 2002 to today, the government has been making the toughening of penal laws into a permanent stock-in-trade, producing a substantial increase in the carceral population. Having been instructed to manage the dramatic consequences of this policy, the CS obtained substantial autonomy in defining the reform it needed.

Nothing seen, nothing heard

In 2006, a prisoner consultation was organized by a group of associations and unions. Their goal, in the context of the Conference on Prison Conditions[27], was twofold: to create a public forum to discuss the prisons question, and to be a platform for addressing the 2007 presidential election candidates. To this end, they relied on the moral authority of former Minister of Justice Robert Badinter. Most importantly, they organized an unprecedented prisoner consultation. A questionnaire was drawn up and then distributed to prisoners to reply anonymously and confidentially. Over 15,000 people replied, almost a quarter of all incarcerated persons in France. Among other things, they spoke of "the misery that can be read in the corner of every eye": "even if we're a pile of muscles, we still have tears in the corners of our eyes"[28].

The day the results of this consultation were published, the organizations taking part in the conference, noticing the very large number of prisoner replies—and before even looking at the results in detail—believed that an important political event had just taken place, shattering the intolerable silence to which the penal system traditionally condemned its subjects, even in periods of reform:

---

27 États généraux de la condition pénitentiaire - All of the documents are available online (in French): www.oip.org.

28 Conference on Prison Conditions, *Cahiers de doléances*, 14 November 2006.

"When a consultation was launched, concerns were raised. Would prisoners reject this chance to express themselves, after their hopes for reform had been dashed so many times? Would they take ownership of a complex, laborious object designed to respect the difficulty of prison issues? Would they react angrily or violently to being offered the chance to express themselves after so much silence? It is clear that prisoners are wondering if the conference will be enough to generate the public and political mobilization that is needed for a radical prison reform, and they expressed this in their answers. It is also clear that this questionnaire was not easy for everyone, as evinced by the example of one prisoner who told us he was answering for himself and friends who did not know how to write. And finally, it is clear that some people's situations were too tragic to accommodate a complex world of proposals, like one person who, under the question asking what he expected from penitentiary reform, only wrote: "help me".

The fact remains that over 15,000 people, or one quarter of the prison population[29], answered our request to create a novel forum on prison conditions. They did it most earnestly, painting a detailed picture of the intolerable aspects of their situation and their hopes for change. Given the opportunity to express themselves politically, they replied with a public-spiritedness that surpasses the shared hopes of an experiment in participatory democracy. This reply should give us an appreciation of the importance of our responsibility to relay their words, which should become a mainspring of reform. Perhaps prior to this, and as a condition of this, their reply must give rise to a revolution in the way we view those whom society has banished and, still today, does not allow to speak.

---

29   This figure is all the more impressive considering the significant level of illiteracy and poor mastery of the French language in detention.

And is this not what prisoners are obviously expecting from us, they who, when asked what they expected from a prison reform, set aside material aspects to express hope of a "change of perspective" from society and more reflection on "penal law"?[30]

There is no doubt much to discuss about the meaning of the results of this consultation. It was about organizations appealing to prisoners with a view to strengthening policy stances favouring less recourse to incarceration and the promotion of prisoners' rights. In this sense, the questionnaire was created to generate discussion on the recommendations of French and European human rights protection authorities. On the basis of this program, a list of demands was drawn up and submitted to the presidential candidates. The conference requested that a penitentiary law be initiated and:

"That this law enshrine custodial sentences as a penalty of last resort, when the offence is so serious that any other penalty or measure would obviously be inadequate.

That this law enshrine the fact that people whose state of health—psychological or physical—is incompatible with detention should be released. If need be, the state must make sure to set up facilities that are suitable for accommodating these people. In particular, offenders with severe psychiatric disorders should be placed in treatment centres adapted to their needs, ensuring their own security and that of third parties.

That this law enshrine the state's respect for the rule of law in prison. The rules in force within the prison system must conform to the principles of a democratic society.

That this law enshrine recognition of all of the fundamental rights and freedoms of prisoners, with

---

30   Conference on Prison Conditions, press release, 20 October 2006.

the exception of the right to come and go, and rights withdrawn through a court decision.

That consequently, this law organize and guarantee the exercise of prisoners' rights to health, hygiene, the maintenance of family connections and social security benefits, education, work, training, as well as social and professional integration. Prisons are an integral part of the country. Public service mandates operate within them according to ordinary legal standards, subject to the constraints inherent to detention. Thus, a prisoner is above all a worker, patient or student in his relationship with his employer, doctor or teacher.

That this law establish that disciplinary penalties can only follow from a decision made under conditions that respect the fair trial principle and are subject to effective remedies; that respect for prisoners' health and dignity are guaranteed during the execution of these penalties.

That this law establish an external oversight body that ensures respect for prisoners' rights, and to which prisoners can appeal in case of violation. That consequently, this body should have the mandate of monitoring general detention conditions, the state of prisons, the application of the prisoner's status, the execution of penitentiary policies. That, consequently, this body should have the power to continually monitor, visit, evaluate, apply injunctions, make recommendations and publish reports.

That this law enshrine the fact that anticipating and preparing for the release of prisoners, and supporting them upon release, are fundamental responsibilities of the Correctional Service. That consequently, a principle should be established according to which the length of prison sentences must take rehabilitation prospects into account.

That this law enshrine the principle that Parliament should evaluate penitentiary policy, nationally and locally, annually and over the long term, giving special attention to detention conditions and prisoner rehabilitation.

That this law recognize the importance of the Correctional Service's role, and enshrine the principle that any prison reform should take particular account of prison staff conditions"[31].

Nicolas Sarkozy admitted that a reform was needed, but unlike candidates of the left and centre, he did not subscribe to the program as a whole. And for a good reason; a central plank of his campaign was a promise to toughen penalties for repeat offenders.

---

31 Etats généraux de la condition pénitentiaire, *Déclaration finale*, 14 November 2006.

CHAPTER 2
Constructing Prisons

The different right-wing Ministers of Justice successively appointed since 2002 have faced many questions about human rights in prisons, from the opposition and occasionally from the majority. To these the same answer is tirelessly given: the plan launched in 2002 to construct 13,200 new places will solve a problem that is ever so worrying in the land of human rights. On 16 June 2008, Rachida Dati, then Minister of Justice, explained that the government's construction policy was a special policy tool to save French prisons from indignity[32]. Equating rights to real estate in this way has the advantage of seeming obvious. In fact, evoking the indignity of the prison system immediately calls to mind two special characteristics. The first is overcrowding (or overpopulation) which represents—quite rightly—both a complete loss of intimacy and the fear of living with strangers in an enclosed space. The second is the combination of dilapidation and insalubrity that are, according to established expressions, reminiscent of living conditions from another time or another place: the Middle Ages, the nineteenth century or the Third World. It is therefore unsurprising to hear the government respond to criticism with the prospect of new, clean prisons, where one person and one person only will have a place in a white cell equipped with a toilet, sink and shower. If you throw in a television, exercise room and two hours of walking, what is left to discuss?

---

32   Rachida Dati on the radio station *France Inter*, Monday 16 June 2008.

And yet behind the obvious, there is a veritable enigma. How can a right, or rights, or respect for people's overall rights find their place between metres of concrete and layers of paint? Something else obvious (something imaginative this time) can be invoked to help us grasp why the rights of incarcerated people cannot be reduced to the material conditions of detention. You are shut up in your home, a home we will imagine is cosy enough. You want to see your family. Too bad they have lived far away ever since you were forced to move by an administrative decision that you were unable to contest before the law. At least your family have come to visit; you have a little time together to say everything you want to say. Too bad someone is listening in on your conversation and observing your effusions. But no matter; you take advantage of the moment, and when the time comes to say goodbye, you head back to your home, reinvigorated. Too bad your walk home is interrupted by a search to check that you have not been given prohibited items, and also too bad that it is a strip-search. Fortunately you can keep affectionate letters with you, under your pillow. Too bad that while you were out, this home of yours was searched as well. But anyway, the letter may already have been read by the CS, just as they read the one you wrote in reply. There is nothing left to do but take refuge in your privacy. At least that is what you think until you notice that the door to your home is pierced by a little hole that makes the space fully visible at all times. If you reflect, something that is favoured by the 22 out of 24 hours spent inside, you will soon understand that accommodation alone does not produce rights.

Inherited discipline

This tale could be long, even endless, because contrary to the confused idea that prison can simultaneously respects people's rights and impose its will to correct, there is an inherent contradiction between discipline and rights. The aim of transforming people, in a context of constraint, entails an irremediable power imbalance. This is what sociologist

Dominique Memmi calls "close domination", when describing how it was challenged in the 1970s (Memmi 2008a; Memmi 2008b). Foucault, in *Psychiatric Power* (Foucault 2008), gives examples of psychiatric treatments based entirely on the substitution of the carer's will for the patient's unreasonable will, by means of the power imbalance inherent in the asylum. The treatment could take advantage of a host of subtleties to be found in the techniques used to impose this will, such as repeatedly causing displeasure as long as submission is not achieved, or granting and withdrawing privileges. As psychiatrist François Leuret explained in 1840 in *Du traitement moral de la folie* (On the Moral Treatment of Insanity): "Let all acts, all manifestations deriving from the illness, that is to say ideas, delirious passions, be followed by a thousand displeasures for the insane person; on the contrary, let all decisions, all behaviour conforming to reason and to the advice of the doctor be compensated" (from Fréminville 1977). This power play cannot escape its initial structure. The patient has been placed in an artificial setting in which everything must work either for or against this substitution of will.

The conflict between discipline and, for example, exercising the right to privacy and to family life is blatantly clear. When prison reformers debate the degree of isolation necessary to get an offender to reflect upon his actions, in one way or another they are deciding the number of personal visits that the prisoner needs or does not need. If isolation is considered conducive to introspection, and contact with friends, family and other prisoners is perceived to be corrupting, it is logical that those responsible for the prisoner's rehabilitation will ration time with family according to their assessment, and not according to the person's right to see his family. Alexis de Tocqueville and Gustave de Beaumont, after touring American prisons, explained the benefits of a regime of strict isolation:

> "There is (...) an undeniable advantage inherent in a
> prison system principally based on isolation; it is that in
> prison, prisoners do not become worse than they were

when they arrived. (...) All moral contagion between prisoners is impossible, especially in Philadelphia, where thick walls separate prisoners day and night. (...) In Philadelphia, the moral situation in which prisoners find themselves is eminently suitable to facilitate their regeneration. (...) This absolute solitude makes the most vivid impression upon all prisoners. One generally finds them ready to open their hearts, and this ability to receive emotions disposes them even more to reform" (Tocqueville 1984, 197-199).

And yet, by using the notion of discipline to understand the totalitarian institution's resistance to the law, one risks an anachronism. If prisoners do not see their families as often as they should, this is no longer because some benefit is expected from isolation. Theoretically, we have done away with the disciplinary objective. Its death warrant was signed by the oft-repeated phrase uttered by Giscard d'Estaing, then French President, in 1974: "Prison is the deprivation of the freedom to come and go, and nothing more". These words obviously expressed a desire to soften prison punishment in its most shocking aspects following the violent riots that had erupted in various prisons from 1972 to 1974, resulting in the deaths of several prisoners. In other words, being in prison does not mean eating vile food, having to respect fussy, infantile rules, submitting to the arbitrariness of the institution and suffering the violence of guards. But taken literally, it was also a formal acknowledgement that the idea of making prison a place of rehabilitation through discipline had been abandoned.

This represented a break with what had, until then, been viewed as an obvious fact: that being deprived of freedom entailed the complete loss of individual rights. The riots were followed by decrees, laws, and amendments to the Code of Criminal Procedure that changed how detention was conceived. They contained notions like the maintenance of family connections, opportunities for contact with the outside world, the right to information, the emergence of social and cultural activities. In 1975, efforts were made to counter the effects of incarceration, for example by improving visiting conditions to better enable the preservation of family ties. Liberalization principles intended to prepare prisoners for release and alleviate their sudden separation from prison were to be temporarily brushed aside by the "security and freedom" law in 1981, which recommended increased penal severity, particularly against perpetrators of violence and repeat offenders (Lazerges 1982). But the dynamic had been set in motion; the Correctional Service was called upon to gradually adapt to the requirements of the principle that the rights of minorities should be standardized and defended throughout society. This standardization groundswell hung over the government, which had made a commitment to human rights and needed to guarantee that they would be applied[33]. Whether it had stemmed from activism or from the European authorities responsible for guaranteeing the application of human rights, the promotion and defence of prisoners' rights led to the introduction of practices that ran counter to system's dominant rationality. The prisoner-as-citizen was now colliding with the dichotomy between "criminal" and "honest man"—the *dividing practice* typical of this rationality (Foucault 2001b; Chantraine 2009a; Chauvenet 2010).

Security pragmatism

That being the case, why is it that thirty years later we are still so far from respecting article 8 of the European Convention on Human Rights, which stipulates that "everyone has the right to respect for his private and family life, his home and his correspondence"? More broadly, how does one explain—to take up a formulation used in a parliamentary report—that "under 'outside' law, everything that is not explicitly prohibited is allowed; under 'inside' law, everything that is not explicitly allowed is prohibited" (Hyest and Cabanel 2000)[34]?

---

33   For example, in 1973 France ratified the European Convention for the Protection of Human Rights and Fundamental Freedoms. On this subject, see Mireille Delmas-Marty (1986).

34   The quote is taken from a chapter meaningfully entitled *"La prison hors le droit"* ("Prison Outside the Law") which takes up the idea that "until the beginning of the 1970s, the idea that prisoners had rights was completely foreign to the Correctional Service".

The persistence of arbitrariness, in parallel with the collapse of correctionalist hopes, had oriented research towards a different analysis of prison system arbitrariness: no longer as a therapeutic aim but as a pragmatic necessity, no longer as an institutional entitlement, but as a way of operating (Faugeron 1996). Far from being organized around a single disciplinary principle, the security imperative and the prisoner containment objective forced the Correctional Service and its agents to manage everyday life pragmatically: on a day-to-day basis they negotiate, repress, grant privileges, exploit, oppress, penalize and reward prisoners, in order to produce a relative lack of disorder in detention (Chantraine 2004).

Security pragmatism, the soundest ideological justification, can be broken down into two complementary principles: maintaining order within the premises and preventing escape. The first principle is based on the realization that the institution is relatively weak compared to its residents, even if only because, in a democratic context, it cannot always ensure order through physical constraint. It has to negotiate, in two ways: through threats and promises. Prisoners are threatened with transfers, disciplinary quarters, isolation, and all of the discretionary harassment possible in a system that is still closed and invisible (for example banging on cell doors during night rounds). Promises take the form of the possibility of little favours (a shower, a cigarette), access to activities and work, contact with family, and above all the prospect of freedom through sentence reductions.

The second principle, which aims to reduce the number of escapes (if this is still an objective at prisons), is employed to varying degrees. It was emphasized less at moments when prisons were being reformed along philanthropic or liberal lines (after 1945, after 1975). It returned to prominence at times when the protective role of incarceration triumphed (for example during the Algerian War, which saw the imprisonment first of Algerian independence activists, then French citizens refusing independence who had formed a group called the *Organisation armée secrète*, OAS [the Secret Army

Organization][35]). Today this principle is guaranteed by a set of security systems (watchtowers, anti-helicopter ropes, metal detectors) and security practices (body searches, cell searches, general searches, and, again, placing prisoners in isolation or in disciplinary quarters, or transferring them). A study into the relationship between escape and security (Davreux et al. 1996) shattered some preconceived notions: the introduction of non-prison contributors does not increase the risk of escape, and costly investment in security does not reduce it. But, as Claude Faugeron observed, "the 'security fantasy' dispenses with any serious reflection upon prison policy, and leads to resource allocations that deprive prisons of facilities they urgently need" (Faugeron 1996).

Today, the twofold security imperative (maintain order, prevent escape) enables us to judge the value of the "new prisons = human rights" equivalence. In 2002, the new Minister of Justice Dominique Perben gave the CS the objective of limiting escapes, reinforcing security on the premises, and increasing the number of prisons. He disregarded the question of prisoners' neglected rights, but considerably enhanced the means of constraining all challenges to the prevailing order. The prisons placed under construction had been designed according to these requirements: ubiquitous security, minimal visiting rooms, neglect of work spaces. They were, therefore, places where violence did not diminish. After examining the state of prisons that had been constructed on the initiative of Albin Chalandon between 1986 and 1988, one study concluded that these premises, "designed with a great deal of concern about security [...] far from being reassuring, seemed to generate a chronic feeling of unease in personnel and prisoners", a consequence of "an atmosphere of latent violence". The result: "in a quite unexpected way", many of the prisoners "view their placement in the establishment as a disciplinary placement" (Pottier 2005).

---

35 In 1963, after two OAS members escaped, De Gaulle reprimanded Prime Minister Pompidou. "The Minister of Justice is not doing his duty", he wrote at the end of a very dry letter in which he pointed out what appeared to him to be a series of "negligences". As a result, the Minister of Justice attempted to inspire in his troops a "fear of escape" culture (Froment 1998).

The same can be said of the next generation of prisons. Large in size, they are sometimes introduced principally for reasons of spatial planning. Geographer Olivier Milhaud showed that when a penitentiary centre with approximately 700 places was opened in Mont-de-Marchan in 2008, this "was not justified as a replacement for the city jail, which held 98 prisoners in May 2008". But local councillors secured strong support from Alain Juppé [former Prime Minister, now mayor of Bordeaux] for the idea of compensating them "for the loss of a squadron from the Mont-de-Marchan military airbase—a cut that had been decided under his government—by opening an oversized prison" (Milhaud 2009). New buildings such as these require construction sites that benefit large public works contractors. But their construction and implementation do not satisfy the economic logic of the punishment industry (Christie 1993), but rather the government's desire to pursue a repressive policy, at the same time using the increase in the number of prisons as a spatial planning tool[36].

A Correctional Service report on prisoners' right to collective expression described the consequences of the structure of these large premises:

> "New establishments constructed as part of the 13,200 program approved in 2002—a program strongly oriented towards large, modern campuses with the most advanced electronic security—are currently showing certain limitations: a lack of stable geographical reference points, the dominance of passive security at the expense of human contact with guards, the difficulty and slowness of internal movements. It is not unusual to hear prisoners in these new establishments saying they miss their former prison, in spite of the sometimes degraded material conditions of their establishment of origin." (Brunet-Ludet 2010).

The General Secretary of a Correctional Service minority trade union that regularly opposes prison policy orientations

---

36   For a critique of the notion of the "Prison-Industrial Complex ", see Loïc Wacquant (2010b).

explains: "These oversized premises make everyone uneasy, including the prisoners. Some of them feel awful even though they are living in a new, clean environment that should be reassuring. Many of them are lacking human relationships and this leads to incidents. In Lyon-Corbas, Mont-de-Marchan, Roanne, there have already been several instances of prisoners refusing to return to their cells"[37]. Denis Dessus, Vice-President of the National Council of the Association of Architects[38], denounced the public-private partnership policy used for the construction of the new prisons, citing the "telling deficiencies of the prisons in Roanne and Mont-de-Marchan"[39]. Both of these perspectives agree with the analysis of the General Inspector of All Places of Deprivation of Liberty on the prison in Lyon-Corbas, particularly concerning the way in which the structure of the new prisons allows little human contact[40]:

"All interviewees met by the inspectors spoke about their unhappiness and about how difficult it was for them to work in this new establishment. Their particularly tense relationship with the prison population contributes greatly to this overall impression of unease. The guards all said that they no longer had the time to chat with prisoners. Relationships have become cold and impersonal, through intercoms and video surveillance. Both sides miss the day-to-day human relationship that had been established in the old jail in Lyon Perrache"[41].

---

37   Céline Verzeletti, "Les grandes prisons créent un malaise", *Ouest-France*, 10 April 2010.

38   *Conseil national de l'ordre des architectes.*

39   Denis Dessus, "L'endettement caché de la France", *Le Monde*, 10 April 2010.

40   Jean-Marie Delarue, "Je suis pessimiste sur le sort de Corbas", *20 minutes*, 11 December 2009.

41   General Inspector of All Places of Deprivation of Liberty, *Rapport de visite de la maison d'arrêt de Lyon-Corbas*, September-Octoberr 2009, http://www.cglpl.fr/wp-content/uploads/2011/01/MA-Lyon-Corbas-version-web.pdf. See also "L'univers carcéral se déshumanise" *Le Journal du dimanche*, 27 July 2010; "De nouvelles prisons plus confortables mais moins humaines", *La Croix*, 23 November 2009; "Pas de diminution des suicides dans les prisons modernes, "désespérantes"", *Agence France Press*, 6 August 2009; "On est arrivés dans une prison propre, sans rats, sans cafards, sans humanité", *LibéLyon*, 25 February 2010; "Nouvelles prisons, ultramoderne solitude", *Libération*, 16 February 2010.

As the inspector says more directly: it is "better to live with cockroaches than without social relations" (Van den Boogaard 2010). In Mont-de-Marchan, this point of view was corroborated by a local consultation group, which expressed concern about the violence reigning in an establishment that some regarded as a "powder keg", and others thought corresponded perfectly with the inspector's pessimistic diagnosis of other new prisons[42]. This is how the person responsible for prison visitors summed up the changes: lack of human contact, fear generated by the anonymity of the large prison, distance between the prison and the prisoner's family, guards who are also isolated, problems organizing release from a prison that is far away from where the prisoner lives.[43].

In the CSA's language, these construction programs are characterized as "humanization" and "modernization". Yet the combination of maintaining order and reinforcing security produces the exact opposite of a system of rights. Let us return to the privacy example. For security reasons, a cell is not a private space. It has to be visible, and can be opened and searched at any time. And a visit from outside without any separation barrier entails the risk of prohibited items being passed, necessitating a body search. Family visits can now take place without a separation barrier, but this is not really a right. It can be suspended by disciplinary action. This means that in a closed system that places its own security above all else, rights do not exist unless the institution is provided with the possibility of control, exemption or withdrawal. This is why the introduction of visiting rooms without security systems was accompanied by an increase in the number of searches and infrared detection systems.

Comparisons with other countries are telling in this regard. Even when the recognition of prisoners' rights is incorporated into the framework of a genuine penitentiary law, as in Belgium (Mary 2006) or in Germany (Mansuy 2005; Salle 2009), the same mechanism is at work. Privileges are then

---

42 Report on the meeting of the Mont-de-Marchan prison local consultative group, 31 March 2010.

43 Interview with the local head of a prison visitors' association, October 2010.

indeed turned into rights, but legal exceptions turn them back into privileges. These new rights are most often only recognized in a small space they have been given at the heart of a security imperative. In other words, this imperative constitutes the fundamental standard before which every subjective right continues to yield way (Chantraine and Kaminski 2007).

Rights policy, or rights politics?

And yet, just because rights in prison tend to adapt to the operation of the institution (that is, to exude their share of arbitrariness), that does not mean they are treated with indifference. It is not a matter of indifference whether the CS sets itself the goal of eliminating escapes and forcibly quelling every gesture of protest, or instead makes room for dialogue and renounces the paranoid vision of an ubiquitous, permanent risk. This is why an internal CS report found that, to curb the tensions created by real estate policies, it was a necessity to make room for conflicts to be discussed:

> "Viewed in the context of the development of the Correctional Service's building policy—involving, on the one hand, large sets of very modern buildings where electronics are gradually replacing the actions and voices of guards (automatic doors, electronic liaison notebooks,[44] to mention only two examples) and, on the other hand, the extension and expansion of outsourcing (work, training, nutrition, laundry, receiving family members)—the question of prisoners formally participating in defining and tracking the rules governing their own care can also be interpreted as a vital necessity for the CS, rather than being seen as a favour granted to the detained person" (Brunet-Ludet 2010).

---

44   An electronic liaison notebook (CEL) is a computerized tool used to record observations on the everyday behaviour of prisoners in detention, and for communication between professionals. This veritable informational panoptic is the subject of lively controversy (it has been subject to legal challenges by International Prison Watch) and intense resistance (by external staff, like nurses who overwhelmingly refuse to write anything in them, despite the constant pressure to which they are subjected in this regard).

The extent to which recommendations such as these are followed remains unclear. For their part, lawyers and activist jurists can use the letter of the law as a weapon against small administrative adjustments. On 25 October 2006, a woman visited her partner on his deathbed. He was under detention at the Fresnes jail hospital. She brought him some small items she hoped would make his last days easier (body cream, soft drinks, disposable razors, postcards). Prison officials noticed these objects and decided to suspend her visitor permit. This was picked up by International Prison Watch, and five days later the administrative court urgently overruled the decision and allowed the person to visit the dying prisoner. It then overruled the decision officially, drawing attention to the fact that the suspension of the visitors permit represented an infringement of the right to carry out a normal family life. Taking the state of the prisoner's health into account, and using European Human Rights Convention terminology, the suspension was characterized as "inhumane and degrading treatment" (Mouazan and de Suremain 2007).

Thus, far from being an experts' debate between prison reformers, the battle for rights extends all the way from the intransparency of the cells and passageways in which the daily resistance against arbitrariness persists, to the oversight and legal formalities of the European Court of Human Rights, passing by way of the national administrative courts, whose judicial precedents are fuelled by prisoner complaints. For example, the European Prison Rules are indispensable to jurisprudential advances at the level of the European Court of Human Rights (ECHR). ECHR judge Françoise Tulkens explained: "The court is increasingly taking into consideration what is accepted in the European Prison Rules. They are important because they convey a European consensus. This consensus is decisive, because if the court proceeds in a solitary and blind manner, member states resist and nothing moves forward. The court also makes increasingly frequent use of the reports of the European Committee for the Prevention of Torture (CPT), which can help substantiate a complaint" (Tulkens 2006).

To appreciate how much the human rights riddle affects our conception of penal justice, one must resist the temptation to simply turn it into "humanitarian" discourse, which, along with "securitarism", "constitute the most widely shared discourses on penitentiaries" (Brossat 2001). It is equally important to refuse to make-believe that rights advance by means of "modernization". The critical task is to hear what is at stake in prisoners' demand for rights:

"Who do I think I am to try to defend my rights? Who do I think I am, this person who did so much harm? That's the question: do I have the right to have rights? Do I have the right to have rights in terms of work? Do I have the right say what I think about a system that, instead of helping us, hopes to break us down and exterminate us? Because without rights there is no dignity, no possibility of relearning the fundamental values of France, which has given us a second chance by supplying an opportunity to really struggle with ourselves. (...) After long years of repentance and reflection, I'm changing course, even if what I did is always at the front of my mind. Now I understand that my actions can't annihilate my rights, because by trying to forget my rights, and by extension my very self, instead of forging ahead with my rehabilitation, I tend to sink into a kind of depression, and take a step backwards. For me, not fighting against an institution that decides and thinks for me amounts to death. And yet I'm not dead, I'm still alive, so I have the right to be human even if I've done the worst. (...) But who do I really think I am? Have no fear, I know where I am, and the situation I'm in, but nothing will silence me. (...) It's about not being satisfied with doing work without rights, designed to keep us busy and push us to buy things, and about not feeling sorry for ourselves but reacting against a prison machine that wants us to rot down to the marrow. Yes, I still have rights".[45]

---

45   Statement by a prisoner, published in *Dedans dehors*, no. 55, May-June 2006.

Showing the political power of this assertion means assessing the extent to which it is both utopian in relation to our punishment practices and a source of endless daily struggle, even in our most modern prisons. This "modernity" is particularly visible in the increasing sophistication of prisoner classification techniques, which we will now examine in detail.

CHAPTER 3
Classifying Prisoners

The "human" and "modern" management of prisoners promoted by the Correctional Service was partly based on renovating prison buildings. But it was also partly based on promoting new ways of dividing up prisoners. In the administration's view, the trends towards recognizing rights and imprisoning more people for longer periods gave it the need for full discretion to classify prisoners and diversify security regimes.

High-security quarters: models and drawbacks

To explain the direction they wanted the reform to take, the CS took up a principle from the 1975 reform that followed the revolts. It defended the idea that it was necessary to link the transformation of prison conditions to the creation of new security regimes based on an assessment of each prisoner's dangerousness. As Philippe Robert explained about the 1975 reform, "to attempt to overcome the perils resulting from carceral overcrowding, we are combining the liberalization of the ordinary regime with the establishment of very strict special regimes" (Robert 1984, 196). These detention regimes, designated as "high-security quarters" or QHS[46], were denounced by activists, then cancelled by the left-wing government that assumed power in 1981. But the Minister of Justice still subscribed to the principle on which QHSs had been founded. A 1993 administrative report denounced

---

"the hindrance of myths and symbols", particularly those surrounding high-security wings "whose symbolic burden is so heavy, it seems to paralyze all serious reflection on the differential treatment of the most dangerous prisoners" (Inspectorate General of the CS and the Inspectorate General of Judicial Services 1993). The CS recently reconsidered the reasons for the failure of this attempt:

> "Perceived abuses in the use of high-security wings led not only to their abolition, but also to the disappearance of all official measures relating to dangerous prisoners, with the exception of the very limited category of Specially Guarded Prisoners[47]. Of course, unofficial lists were created *ipso facto*, since the implementation of rehabilitation programs is conditional on the evaluation of the dangerousness of prisoners" (Direction de l'administration pénitentiaire 2007).

In this surprisingly candid passage, the CS acknowledged that the creation of differential security regimes, which had been curbed since high-security wings had been abandoned, operated outside of any legislative framework. And in the process of apparently lamenting it, the CS indicated that "pressure groups were able to skilfully exploit the impact of illegal acts committed by the administration by bringing all classification into question."

The Correctional Service drew a clear contrast between the desire to classify prisoners and recognition of equal rights: "For the sake of an egalitarian approach to prisoners, which limits the possibility of creating categories, for the sake of its non-predictability, which precludes us from considering that such-and-such characteristic would predispose a person to such-and-such behaviour, it was impossible for us to create a real prisoner classification system, and yet this is the foundation of any differential regime worthy of the name" (Direction de l'administra-

---

47   *Détenus particulièrement surveillés.*

tion pénitentiaire 2007). In fact, the attempt to recreate differential detention regimes outside the law made the CS vulnerable. For example, in 2007, the administrative tribunal in Nantes approved legal oversight of decisions made in this context, exposing the legal foundations of these CS decisions to scrutiny, and therefore to censure. This meant that at any moment, a judge needing to understand an individual decision could perceive the system's illegality. This is why the penitentiary law was designed to shield prison management from procedural formalities and judicial oversight. In the CS's view, reform could only extend the institution's subjection to the supervision of the law and the courts, without at the same time equipping it with distinct detention regimes and legitimate means of justifying transfers between these.

In making its case for classification, the CS tried to superimpose two justifications. The first took up the old correctionalist idea that detention regimes needed to be adapted to prisoners' personalities. In contemporary terms, this is saying that classification is "the precondition for rehabilitation". This argument poorly masks the predominance of a second argument, borrowed from the rhetoric that accompanied the 1975 reforms, which resulted in the creation of high-security wings: under order to respect new rights, the CS responded that distinguishing prisoners was a necessity. The separation of troublesome prisoners was presented as the very condition of reform. This claim shows the institution's characteristic way of integrating rights, which is to immediately anticipate possibilities for dispensation, that is, for maintaining order through the preservation of discretionary power.

Risk management as a punishment rationale

The law that reached Parliament in March 2009 therefore represented the prison Correctional Service's conception of what was acceptable as well as the management methods it wanted to promote. In this context, it is not easy to link the bill to any tradition of thought on the purpose of punishment. During the parliamentary debates, different conceptions of prison reform emerged within the majority. Before even speaking about the bill, Rachida Dati, then Minister of Justice, said that "since 2002 in fact, unprecedented efforts have been made to modernize our prisons. In 2009, the delivery of nine new establishments has created 5,000 additional places"[48]. Like many other MPs, she depicted the increase in the number of prisons as a central means of acting in the interest of prisoners. At the beginning of the debates, UMP deputy Christian Vanneste took a hard line on security, explaining that "a society that believes in its values should not be ashamed of punishing those who transgress them"[49]. This formulation conflicted with the government's depiction of the bill, with its emphasis on the law's ambitions in terms of rights recognition and rehabilitation. For example, Michèle Alliot-Marie said: "The bill also aims to address the loopholes and inadequacies—we need to be able to recognize reality and call it what it is—of the penitentiary law"; "from the moment they are imprisoned, prisoners should stick to a personalized penal process under which they can develop, heal and work"[50]. In the course of the debates, when the parliamentary left challenged the law's shortcomings, speakers from the majority oscillated between defending the bill's ambition and presenting it as being consistent with existing penal policy, which was based on increasing the number of prisons and reaffirming the punitive purpose of penalties.

But these contradictory positions on the overall purpose of punishment gave way to what, for the Minister of Justice, was "the crux" of the reform[51]. This resulted from linking two articles of the law.

---

48   Michèle Alliot-Marie, National Assembly, 15 September 2009.
49   Christian Vanneste, National Assembly, 15 September 2009.
50   Michèle Alliot-Marie, National Assembly, 15 September 2009.
51   An expression used by the director of Correctional service administration in a letter addressed to regional directors, 18 September 2009.

Article 22

The Correctional Service guarantees all prisoners respect for their dignity and their rights. The exercise of these cannot be subject to restrictions other than those resulting from the inherent constraints of detention, from the maintenance of security and good order in the establishments, from the prevention of recidivism and from the protection of victim's interests. These restrictions take into account the age, state of health, disabilities and personality of the detained person.

Article 89

The placing of convicts in prisons established for the purpose of punishment is conducted with consideration for their penal category, age, state of health and personality. Their detention regime is determined taking account of their personality, health, dangerousness and social rehabilitation efforts. The placing of a prisoner under a more strict detention regime would not infringe the rights provided for under article 22 of penitentiary law number 2009-1436 of 24 November 2009.

Article 22 sets forth an imperative to respect rights and then lists reasons permitting their derogation. Its drafting was thus described by jurist Martine Herzog-Evans: "A very vague and summary proclamation of rights ("their rights", is that it?) and dignity is followed by a run-on sentence and a second sentence authorizing their infringement for motives as vague and compassionate as the internal order of the establishments. Moreover, this text serves as a prop for differential regimes [...], reinforcing the idea that they have the effect of limiting people's rights and dignity" (Herzog-Evans 2010). Article 89 formalizes the idea of differential detention regimes and can, without contradiction—in light of the exceptions provided for under article 22—assert that these different regimes do not undermine respect for rights. Rachida Dati explained that "the establishment of differential regimes within the same prison has no effect on prisoners' rights"[52].

The rationale that links penal reforms to penitentiary reforms has one important fault. It rests on a fiction, namely the identification of breaches of the prison order with the risk of recidivism. This connection falls apart if we consider, for example, that although people convicted of sexual offences are symbols of dangerousness in society—something that justifies the use of multiple evaluations to assess their risk level—they are also people who present few disciplinary problems in prison. By confusing conformance to prison standards with the absence of risk for society, risk management draws a fictional line of continuity between order inside prison and security outside.

However, this was not easy to challenge. The lack of an alternative prison theory from the opposition in Parliament, in the context of what the government presented as a long-awaited law that required consensus, created some confusion over strategies for debating the bill. The government used the penitentiary law's mere arrival before legislators as a sign of openness and balance, a counterpoint to its policy of penal severity. The bill was presented as *the* penitentiary law, not as a reform but as *the* bill everyone had been waiting for, which they—unlike the socialist government in power from 1997 to 2002—had had the courage to submit to Parliament. This view was hard for the left to counter, for several reasons. First, because they in fact never stopped asking for such a law to be placed on the agenda. When it was shelved from 2002 to 2007, they had taken this as the clearest sign of the Right's lack of interest in the issue. Second, because they also saw this as an opportunity that should be seized. The scarcity of legislative debates on the prison system was an incentive to work on improving a bill that would probably be impossible to rescind by means of a later law. In June 2008, former Minister of Justice Marylise Lebranchu concluded that the bill "contains advances, for both staff and prisoners". At the

---

52   Rachida Dati, Senate, 5 March 2009.

opening of the debates following important amendment work by the senator who had introduced the bill, former socialist Minister of Justice Robert Badinter said he was convinced the bill would be "a big law"[53]. After the law was passed by the Senate, a group of associations launched an appeal, entitled "Prison in Search of a Consensus"[54]. It was designed to hinder both left-wing critics and members of the majority in the National Assembly who might have been tempted to go back on concessions passed by the Senate.

One reason why some members of the opposition took this consensualist approach to the bill was that, although the parliamentary left's line of opposition was—with a few exceptions—clear on the matter of the government's *penal* policy, some of its members subscribed to a conceptual framework shared with the majority on what could be done in terms of *prison* policy. This framework could be found in the left's own aborted legislative elaborations. Even though a private member's bill tabled in 2003 by socialist deputies had brought this position into the light of day, the left attempted to deny its significance through a series of rhetorical shifts. As that bill had explained:

"The classification of penal establishments would not rest on a division of prisoners according to the quantum or remainder of their sentences, but rather on legally predetermined objective criteria that would enable the convicts' situations and personalities to be assessed. This assessment would be carried out throughout their detention so that prisoners' classifications could be adapted to their personal development."[55]

This text is interesting because it evinces its authors' theoretical discomfort. It recognizes the need for estab-

53   Robert Badinter, Senate, 3 March 2010.
54   Collective, "La prison à la recherche d'un consensus", September 2009, http://appel. loipenitentiaire.fr/.
55   *Proposition de loi sur la peine et le service public pénitentiaire*, submitted by left-wing deputies, recorded by the Presidency of the National Assembly on 25 June 2003.

lishment classification, and aims to give the classification system a foundation that will make it less arbitrary, contrary to the rights recognition that constitutes the backbone of the proposal. This is the reason why the text emphasizes that any criteria replacing those based on sentence length should be "objective" and "legally predetermined", and that they should correspond to "the convicts' situations and personalities". It overlooks something that presents a problem: the subjective and questionable character of personality evaluation, which contrasts with the goal of legal objectivity and certainty. This kind of affirmation/denial mechanism also came fully into play when left-wing deputies described the consequences of classifying establishments:

> "These establishments would have different security levels. However, this difference would only affect the organization of prison life within the strict limits of security requirements. The highest security level should not deprive prisoners of rights otherwise asserted, but should instead enable them to exercise these under optimal conditions, taking their personality into account. The definition of a higher security level can involve, beyond just special building facilities (watchtowers, higher outer walls...), a greater number of guards and social workers to enable activities to be run efficiently. Classification according to security level could be applied not only to the whole establishment, but also—where premises allow—within individual establishments"[56].

This type of formulation—which asserts that placement in a high-security prison would be conducive to the exercise of rights because the establishment would be adapted to the person—would appear to be rather counter-intuitive, when one considers the real consequences of being placed in high-security establishments, and that these placements

---

56   *Ibidem.*

are often the result of disputed administrative decisions. This euphemization is also partly contradicted by formulations that concern not prisons this time, but jails: "In addition to the maintenance of sub-regional jails, the law provides for the establishment of regional jails that would house people who pose a significant risk to the order and security of the establishment, and those whose personalities warrant special monitoring. This will result in more prison staff, more vigilance and more restrictive treatment by personnel". Here the proposal states the reality of its project more clearly: management according to risk, resulting in differential methods of restraint.

Making the rights policy public

This line of thinking was not shared by all of the MPs who participated in the debates in the Senate and the National Assembly. As a result of rights protection organizations and bodies having formalized the imperatives of a penitentiary policy that promotes rights, these imperatives emerged in Parliament as a kind of opposition to the CS's plans. In a way, during the discussion of the bill—which the opposition considered very deceptive—this appropriation by the opposition was the real political event. Contrary to the government's idea that the creation of differential regimes had no impact on respect for rights, senator Alain Anziani (Socialist Party) believed that differential regimes "exude arbitrariness".[57]. To counter this risk of arbitrariness, he requested that "all references to dangerousness be removed from the bill": "The notion of dangerousness is vague. Who's dangerous? For whom? For what? According to which criteria? This is all quite unclear."[58]. Socialist deputy Jean-Jacques Urvoas resumed this line of criticism in the Assembly: "Introducing this sort of system would amount to abolishing all reference to any general, impersonal standard which the prisoner could demand to

---

57   Alain Anziani, Senate, 3 March 2009.
58   Alain Anziani, Senate, 5 March 2009.

have respected. And all of this just serves to establish a shifting, fluctuating regime that satisfies only the requirements of the Correctional Service"[59]. He insisted that "a fundamental right must remain a fundamental right, including in prison".

The left's contribution to the legislative debate, therefore, mixed two tenors. The first aimed to improve a bill whose administrative foundation was not being criticized enough. The second gave voice to those who were critical of the power granted to the CS to define detention regimes and define the rules for assigning them to prisoners. The Right likened this criticism to a direct attack on the CS. Jean-Paul Garraud thought it amounted to "a kind of trial against the Correctional Service"[60]. The left responded by drawing attention to the recommendations of rights protection bodies and associations. Jean-Jacques Urvoas mentioned the opinion of the CNCDH, which had expressed its opposition to legalizing a system that it said would be certain to "dramatically increase the administration's power over incarcerated individuals and very clearly raise the risk of arbitrariness"[61]. He quoted Thomas Hammarberg, the European Council's Commissioner for Human Rights, who, in a memorandum submitted after his visit to France in May 2008, let it be it known that he would be keeping an eye on the situation to ensure that "the establishment of differential detention regimes would not be legalized"[62]. Deputy Michel Vaxès (French Communist Party) summed up the view of observers who were disappointed by the reform: "You gave us an appointment with history; it's a missed appointment. And yet, Correctional Service unions, judges and lawyers, associations and contributors, International Prison Watch, institutions including the CNCDH and the General Inspector of All Places of Deprivation of Liberty arrived on time for this important appointment. Along with them, we are deeply disappointed"[63].

---

59   Jean-Jacques Urvoas, National Assembly, 15 September 2009.
60   Jean-Paul Garraud, National Assembly, 15 September 2009.
61   Jean-Jacques Urvoas, National Assembly, 15 September 2009.
62   *Ibidem.*
63   Michel Vaxès, National Assembly, 15 September 2009.

The left voted against the law in the Assembly but abstained in the Senate. The opposition distanced itself from previous reform bills and took up the criticism of differential regimes in the name of the protection of rights. This new development marked the end of the majority's will to reach a political consensus on the reform. In counterpoint, the parliamentary right defined its law not so much as a digression from the policy battle that should have united the parties around shared objectives, but as a continuation of its penal policy. The risk rhetoric served to establish this continuity. Michèle Alliot-Marie more directly acknowledged the legal consequences of differential detention regimes, claiming that it would "put an end to the unjust, ineffective egalitarianism that has prevailed until recently"[64]. The notion of dangerousness became a bridge between the apparently contradictory meanings of the penal and penitentiary laws. This was the position of Jean-Paul Garraud, the UMP deputy who introduced the bill to the Assembly. He was one of the most vehement defenders of preventive detention[65]. This is how he characterized the consistency between penal reforms and penitentiary reforms:

> "To be able to mend one's ways, one must first recognize one's mistake, and in this sense punishment has a pedagogical value, a deterrent and exemplary value. This must go in both directions: on the one hand, differential regimes based specifically on dangerousness and, on the other, a full range of sentence adjustments placed at the disposal of the judicial authority, which assesses rehabilitation guarantees and the absence of the risk of recidivism case-by-case" [66].

One important detail is that Jean-Paul Garraud did not present the question of risk management as a *risk reduction* factor but as a *risk elimination* factor. He said it elsewhere

---

64   Michèle Alliot-Marie, National Assembly, 15 September 2009. This rhetoric denouncing "egalitarianism" is part of a broader criticism of the "heritage" of "May 68", whose "elimination" Nicolas Sarkozy has called for. See Serge Audier (2008).

65   We will address the law on secure detention in more detail in chapter 5.

66   Jean-Paul Garraud, National Assembly, 15 September 2009.

even more clearly: "At the conjunction of numerous imperatives that might seem contradictory, the prison system is developing, and it must also get its prisoners to develop towards a rehabilitation that excludes all risk of recidivism"[67]. This desire to exclude all risk of recidivism was to specifically result in the promulgation of the secure detention law—to be explored in chapter 5—and potentially the transformation of the meaning and application of sentence adjustments, sparking a new set of political controversies, which we will now reconstruct and analyse.

---

67   *Ibidem.*

CHAPTER 4
Managing flows

A nother section of the penitentiary law dealt with the adjustment of prison sentences. This penal component had no direct link with the law's strictly penitentiary aspect, and it belonged to a different timeframe. It was the extension of the right-wing majority's 2004 attempt to create a new sentence adjustment procedure (known as the NPAP[68]). The aim of this reform, like that of 2009, was to increase the number of adjusted sentences by encouraging the use of administrative procedures instead of individualized, judicial procedures. The 2009 reform grew out of the failure of the 2004 reform which, in practice, had scarcely been applied by judicial actors[69]. The reasons that had made it necessary remained. Much like in 2002, the 2007-2012 legislature began with the passing of a penal law and a rise in the carceral population. The law of 10 August 2007 was intended to force judges to apply minimum sentences to repeat offenders. One way of managing the penitentiary consequences (carceral overpopulation) of this penal policy (carceral population growth) was to encourage the early release of prisoners.

---

68   NPAP stands for *nouvelle procédure d'aménagement de peine*, literally "new sentence adjustment procedure".

69   This is what centrist senator Jean-René Lecerf described in his report on the penitentiary law: "Essentially, the most substantial changes concern the procedure applicable to convicts at the end of their sentences, known in 2004 as the "new sentence adjustment procedure" or even the "exit valve", which, as the senator who presented the bill has already indicated in his general presentation, did not have the expected effects", Jean-René Lecerf, *Rapport sur le projet de loi pénitentiaire*, a report prepared on behalf of the Senate law commission, 17 December 2008.

But the wisdom of this drive was subject to debate, not only within the ruling government, but also in Parliament and among professional organizations. Here, the dividing line was somewhat askew. The part of the law that dealt with sentence adjustment created a clash between, on the one hand, the administrative pragmatism demanded by the government and supported by the left in the interest of reducing prisoners' incarceration time and, on the other hand, proponents (MPs, police, community activists) of increased penal severity, not only at the time of sentencing but also during its execution.

Two central ideas enter into competition as soon as the subject of sentence adjustment comes under discussion. On the one hand there is the idea that adjustments have proven more effective in terms of recidivism prevention than end-of-sentence releases and that, simultaneously, these should enable carceral overcrowding to be effectively counteracted. On the other hand, every serious repeat offence committed by an early-release prisoner is turned into an opportunity to discuss prolonging sentences, and resurrects the idea that prison should first and foremost serve a neutralizing function. It also revives the idea that, where the most serious crimes are concerned, this objective makes it necessary to consider the legal possibility of confinement *ad vitam aeternam*, including after the end of the original sentence. The CNCDH, giving an account of the difficulty of implementing the Council of Europe's[70] penal policy recommendations, described the authorities' general attitude towards the range of alternatives to detention:

"In response to the recommendations of European bodies, French authorities have very often taken an ambivalent attitude. On the one hand they encourage the use of incarceration as the only penal solution when dealing with acts they wish to publicly condemn, going as far as denouncing the lack of imprisonment

---

70   Council of Europe, *Recommendation concerning prison overcrowding and prison population inflation*, 1999; Council of Europe, *Recommendation on Conditional Release (Parole)*, 2003; Council of Europe, *Recommendation on the management by prison administrations of life sentence and other long-term prisoners*.

as though this amounted to the absence of a penalty. On the other hand, leaders of all kinds also desire, though more discreetly, to develop alternatives to detention whose benefits they know in terms of recidivism prevention and lower financial costs" (CNCDH 2007b).

This ambivalence can be characterized by three elements. First, sentence adjustments and increased penal severity are promoted simultaneously. Second, the willingness to develop these measures is linked to increasing prison capacity. Finally, within the sentence adjustment procedures themselves, a central place is given to the use of electronic bracelets, which are conceived both as an adjustment and as a means of pursuing detention outside the prison walls—in other words, as a specific form of penal net-widening (Cohen 1985).

A development desired by the government

In the process of preparing the penitentiary reform, the development of sentence adjustments was initially placed among the bill's explicit objectives. Rachida Dati, then Minister of Justice, in her speech at the July 2007 inauguration of the Restricted Steering Committee (RSC) responsible for preparing the reform, said that "the question of sentence adjustment is essential for two reasons: first, as I have said, because it should be assumed that no human being should be committed to spending the rest of his life deprived of freedom; second, because we must be pragmatic, and take account of the fact that prison is not necessarily the right answer for all convicted criminals. In this context, prolonged retention in prison may not be the best guarantee against recidivism"[71].

The Restricted Steering Committee attempted to respond to these questions by arguing, in a general sense, in favour of sentence adjustments:

---

71   Rachida Dati, steering committee inaugural speech, 11 July 2007.

"Only sentence adjustment—*ab initio* [in other words with regard to convicts at liberty] for short sentences, or in the second phase of the execution of longer sentences—has what it takes to respond to the twofold objective of lasting prisoner rehabilitation (a prime factor in the fight against recidivism) and reparation for damages suffered by the victim of the offence. In order for sentence reductions to establish a contract with convicts formalizing the avenues and means of executing their sentences, a proactive, credible policy is required. This must be based on mobilizing the appropriate social aids and organizations to respond to the needs of individual situations where necessary, as well as on a more effective monitoring process to make sure the obligations that come with sentence reductions are being met." (COR 2007).

Concretely, the committee proposed a series of reforms, including: for all convicts (even repeat offenders), setting the middle of the sentence as the time when parole could be requested; more non-prison sentence adjustment possibilities; implementing a new system that would automatically adjust the final three months of custodial sentences of two years or less (COR 2007), etc. Some of these recommendations provided the framework for the sentence adjustment reforms proposed to lawmakers in the Senate. The three principal innovations proposed concerned a reform of the approval procedure, assigning a new role to the Rehabilitation and parole services (SPIP), the systematization of releasing prisoners fitted with electronic bracelets during the final months of their sentences, and the extension from one to two years of sentences that are subject to the possibility of either being adjusted or being served entirely in open detention.

In the spring of 2009, the government began promoting the principle of sentence adjustment before Parliament during the debate on the penitentiary law. In the Senate, Rachida Dati said that recidivism prevention "with sentence adjustments" was a "crucial issue"[72]. Michèle Alliot-Marie, who had become Minister of Justice, took up this plea in the National Assembly in the autumn of 2009: "Dry releases—when prisoners find themselves left to their own devices after being released from prison, like you see in some films—are not a good solution. It is always preferable to anticipate release, particularly because it gives prisoners a chance to think about what will happen after their release and prepare for it" [73].

These formulations of principle were approved by a number of opposition MPs who were otherwise critical of the penitentiary element of the bill[74]. Former Minister of Justice Elizabeth Guigou believed that "dry releases, without preparation, are conducive to recidivism" [75]. To her, "the solution lies in sentence adjustment: electronic bracelets, semi-releases, paroles, external placements that allow a transition between prison and the outside. As for short sentences, it would be better if they were served somewhere other than prison"[76]. Robert Badinter said he supported "these interesting measures"[77]. On behalf of the Communist Party in the Senate, Nicole Borvo Cohen-Seat explained: "We can only applaud the advances made in the area of sentence adjustments, since this is something we care about deeply"[78].

A penal policy rupture?

In spite of these consensual declarations of principle, the MPs were still a long way from agreement on the details of the law itself, and on the how it should fit into the government's penal policy. The first level of disagreement concerned how these new measures broke with the policy that had been pursued since 2002. Robert Badinter supported the sentence adjustment provisions because

---

72   Rachida Dati, Senate, 3 March 2009.
73   Michèle Alliot-Marie, National Assembly, 15 September 2009.
74   See the chapter 3.
75   Elizabeth Guigou, National Assembly, 15 September 2009.
76   *Ibid.*
77   Robert Badinter, Senate, 6 March 2009.
78   Nicole Borvo Cohen-Seat, Senate, 6 March 2009.

they "marked a true break with the policy that has been pursued up until now"[79]. He specifically pointed to the fact that "even repeat offenders will be able to benefit, and this is not exactly in the spirit of the law that was passed"[80]—the one that established minimum sentences. According to Socialist senator Alain Anziani, "here there is a real contradiction, which we have pointed out on several occasions: there's no use filling prisons to the brim if we then go out of our way to empty them, using means that are more secretive, especially in the eyes of the public"[81]. Communist senator Nicole Borvo Cohen-Seat denounced "the incompatibility between the government's previous policy and the bill that we are considering today. How can we be favouring alternative punishments and prisoner support with a view to rehabilitation after having considerably toughened conditions for obtaining conditional release, the social utility of which has been proven time and again?"[82]. Similarly, former socialist Minister of Justice Marylise Lebranchu wondered: was it not "time to recognize that we will regulate carceral overpopulation by dealing not with the problem of releases, but with that of admissions?"[83].

The debate concentrated on the measure to create more *ab initio* sentence adjustment possibilities, and on how this measure related to the penal policy as a whole. The accusation of inconsistency was of course refuted by Rachida Dati in the Senate: "You say there is a contradiction in the penal policy. No, there is complementarity"[84]. But the question reverted to the National Assembly. Then it was no longer a case of opposition lawmakers denouncing inconsistency while at the same time supporting—for better or for worse—what they deemed to be a step forward, but rather of majority deputies refusing to pass a bill that seemed to

---

79   Robert Badinter, Senate, 6 March 2009.
80   *Ibid.*
81   Alain Anziani, Senate, 6 March 2009.
82   *Ibid.*
83   Marylise Lebranchu, National Assembly, 15 September 2009.
84   Rachida Dati, Senate, 6 March 2009.

them to go back on the guiding lines of their repressive penal policy. This debate resumed after the Minster of the Interior received a warning from police union leaders, who let it be known that they were opposed to some of the bill's provisions. On September 1 2009, the secretary-general of *Union Synergie Officers* wrote that he "vigorously denounced the inconsistency and duplicity of a system that will no longer execute judicial decisions, showing no respect for citizens and victims"[85]. The union believed that the aim of the sentence adjustment proposal was to surreptitiously undo the public work of justice: "Justice that is visible and interpretable by those subject to trial in France will be handed down by the criminal court, which will determine the required sentence, and then this will be discreetly reviewed in the office of the penalty enforcement judge, until a parole is granted pure and simple"[86]. The secretary-general drew attention specifically to the question of repeat offenders and the inconsistency between the bill under consideration and the law passed in August 2007: "The bill does not exempt repeat offenders from these measures, and this conflicts with the president's desire to penalize them more harshly through minimum sentences. And yet these very repeat offenders and multiple offenders are the ones who are poisoning criminal statistics and the life of the French people"[87].

Similar criticism came from the Institute for Justice. This organization, founded by the father of a murder victim, campaigns for tougher penal and penitentiary policies and is very active in lobbying deputies[88]. It too denounced sentence adjustment as back-room justice, as opposed to public, democratic justice: "No one can deny the elitist and antidemocratic character of this sort of system, quite apart from the fact that

---

85   Bruno Beschizza, "Letter to Brice Hortefeux", 1 September 2009.
86   *Ibid.*
87   *Ibid.*
88   Caroline Monnot, "L'intense lobbying de l'Institut pour la justice en faveur de lois plus répressives", *Le Monde,* 10 October 2010; Laurence De Charrette "Justice: des "citoyens" se lancent dans le lobbying", *Le Figaro,* 23 September 2009; Sonya Faure, "Un Institut pour la justice au lobbying très adroit", *Libération,* 15 September 2009.

it is not a good cause"[89]. The association believed the system would hinder the fight against crime. In its view, on the one hand, "it has never been proven that parole is an effective tool against recidivism, since the people who are selected for early release are precisely those who present the lowest risk of relapse"[90]. On the other hand, "sentence adjustment undermines the presumed symbolism of the sentence"[91].

A short time before the National Assembly began considering the bill passed by the Senate, this criticism received publicity when a police memorandum appeared in the press, warning that the bill could have a "boomerang effect" on crime figures[92]. The Minister of the Interior subsequently spoke of his "vigilance" with regard to the bill[93]. The memorandum in question—which linked a one-year decrease in prisoner numbers to an increase in crime (particularly the 12% rise in burglaries)—was never "found again"[94]. But the arguments it put forward were taken up by some members of the parliamentary majority, forcing the government to negotiate a compromise on the wording of the provision dealing with the adjustment of sentences of two years or less, and to change how it formulated the principles and rationale behind its legislation.

No sooner passed than challenged

The compromise mainly involved imposing restrictions on the reform of article 723-15, by excluding repeat offenders from the extension of qualifying sentences to two years. This was made necessary by opposition to the initial bill from deputies like Claude Bodin, a member of the *Popular Right*, which assembles the UMP's most conservative fringe. He

89   Institute for Justice, Analysis of the Penitentiary Bill, *Etudes et analyses de l'Institut pour la justice*, March 2009.
90   *Ibid.*
91   *Ibid.*
92   "Policiers et gendarmes inquiets de 'l'effet boomerang' des aménagements de peine", *AFP*, 3 September 2009.
93   "Hortefeux sera 'vigilant' sur la discussion de la prochaine loi pénitentiaire", *AFP*, 3 September 2009.
94   Isabelle Mandraud, "L'introuvable note policière sur la loi pénitentiaire", *Le Monde*, 11 September 2009.

based his position on the principle that all sentences needed to be fully served: "The best means of preventing recidivism is to impose penalties. Statistics like those presented by the National Crime Monitoring Centre[95] show that six out of ten minors who serve time in prison do not reoffend. It is also an obligation owed to victims and a duty of society"[96]. Jean-Paul Garraud, who presented the bill, backed the idea of excluding repeat offenders, for the sake of being consistent with existing penal policy[97]. Michèle Alliot-Marie proposed a compromise position, which excluded repeat offenders from the raising of the maximum sentence eligible for an *ab initio* adjustment, since it would not, she explained, "be consistent to allow reoffenders to benefit from a sentence adjustment when two years ago this house passed a law that created a minimum sentence system intended to increase sentences for reoffenders"[98]. This compromise made it possible for the law to be passed, but it did not completely quell the conflicts that had been generated on the right. Some deputies of the UMP's right-wing fringe used the police union's argument to challenge the principle of expanding the application of sentence adjustments; Eric Ciotti wondered: "how does one explain that a sentence handed down publicly by a criminal court judge can be discreetly distorted by another judge"[99]? Other MPs tried to fuel their colleagues' doubts by pointing out that they were in fact preparing to pass legislation that the opposition would not have disavowed. This occasionally led to exchanges between partially reversed political

---

95   *Observatoire national de la délinquance.*
96   Claude Bodin, National Assembly, 15 September 2009. In a similar vein, Martine Au-rillac, National Assembly, 15 September 2009: "Measures that provide for the improve-ment of prisoners' living conditions and the replacement, where possible, of detention by sentence adjustments constitute a real step forward in relieving prisons of trial de-fendants as well as convicts with short sentences, and remedying the non-execution of sentences. But we all know that, in an imperfect world, the risk of recidivism is hardly reduced by an electronic bracelet, the tracking of which can be inconsistent. (…) On several occasions we have seen this sadly demonstrated. Therefore it seems to me that the two-year threshold can only be maintained if we exclude from the system repeat of-fenders—a measure that you have approved, Madame minister—and sexual offenders. Our commission happily called for this".
97   Jean-Paul Garraud, National Assembly, 15 September 2009.
98   Michèle Alliot-Marie, National Assembly, 15 September 2009.
99   Eric Ciotti, National Assembly, 15 September 2009.

fronts, some opposition deputies feeling compelled to argue in support of the government's reform against a segment of the majority[100].

This dissent from within the parliamentary Right also led the government to reformulate the rationale of its legislation. Michèle Alliot-Marie explained that it was not so much a matter of decreasing penal severity as ensuring that sentences were better executed. In other words, it was not so much a matter of innovating by changing sentence execution methods as rationalizing sentence execution management in a context of limited prison space:

> "We should therefore look into the use of alternative or complementary penalties. In fact, each year, 30,000 convictions handed down by judges are not executed [...] often due to an insufficient number of places in prisons. Sometimes a figure of 82,000 convictions is cited, but we must distinguish between flow and stock, since some sentences are served several months after being handed down. Of course, this is not a very good thing, but what is worse is that some sentences are not served at all. In that case, not only do sentences lack all pedagogical meaning for the person in question, or lack any deterrent effect on his companions, but the victim has the feeling that justice has not done its work and, finally, it is your credibility, my fellow deputies, and that of the justice system that are at stake"[101].

In saying this, she took up the argument that the legislation would make judicial decisions less effective and turned it upside down to her advantage. She was reviving the polemical theme of unexecuted penalties, originally raised in 2000 when the judges' majority trade union published its *White Paper on Sentence Execution* (USM 2000). French President Nicolas Sarkozy took up the same

100   National Assembly, 17 September 2009.
101   Michèle Alliot-Marie, National Assembly, 15 September 2009.

theme before the Congress on 22 June 2009: "How can we speak of justice when there are 82,000 unserved sentences due to an insufficient number of prison places?"[102] Similarly, at the beginning of 2011, new UMP president Jean-François Copé spoke of "the question of sentence application, whose corollary is the lack of prison places. We are 20,000 short. So we must step up the construction of prison places"[103].

The second change in the justification of the law, brought about in response to criticism from the Right, touched on the very definition of sentence adjustment and consisted in stressing the custodial nature of end-of-sentence measures. The clause that allows short and medium sentences to be systematically served outside prison wearing an electronic bracelet was no longer presented as a release from detention. According to the minister: "Automatic placement under surveillance is not a sentence adjustment; it is, in a sense, a new detention regime"[104]. For Jean-Paul Garraud, this point was precisely what made the system acceptable[105]. The release of prisoners fitted with an electronic bracelet was recast as a sentence execution method, that is, as a measure that transfers the functions of prison outside the walls.

Moreover, the government was considering altering some measures in the bill that offered real possibilities for decreasing incarceration time. In fact, after the law was passed, Brice Hortefeux, then Minister of the Interior, invoked the same argument used by the police unions and the majority's right-wing fringe:

8 December 2010: "Then Brice Hortefeux returned to the subject of the penitentiary law passed in 2009, which he believed contained 'very good things' though adding that 'improvements could be made'.

---

102   Nicolas Sarkozy, "Déclaration de M. le Président de la République devant le Parlement réuni en congrès", Versailles, 22 June 2009.
103   Jean-François Copé, *Le Parisien*, mardi 1 February 2011.
104   Michèle Alliot-Marie, National Assembly, 15 September 2009.
105   Jean-Paul Garraud, National Assembly, 15 September 2009.

[...] The minister finds it 'unhealthy' that an individual sentenced to two years in prison 'that is, for acts that are not minor', should be 'guaranteed not to serve a single day in prison' as is the case today"[106].

Ironically, little noticed in the public debate, Brice Hortefeux twice felt compelled to deplore the excessive severity of the justice system. The first time was on behalf of the police. He considered "disproportionate"[107] the punishment imposed on officers convicted of having provided false testimony in order to incriminate a person they had assaulted. Then it was on his own behalf, in December 2010, after being convicted by a court of first instance for a second time. The first time, he was fined for "racist insults" towards a UMP activist during the party's "summer university". The second time, he was found guilty of having infringed the presumption of innocence of a judge accused of having leaked information about a political scandal to journalists"[108].

But, more seriously, this challenge shows the two platforms on which penal politics are performed. In the media and in the court of public opinion, the proposals considered most effective are those promising more security through increased penal severity. But the concrete management of these proposals is problematic for the prison system. This is why these laws need to be supplemented by technical systems that make it possible, at the other end of the penal chain, to cut prison time short for people seen to present little danger. An arrangement of this kind is always at the mercy of publicity; proponents of penal severity can seize upon it and present it to the public as a sign of weakness.

106   Brice Hortefeux, "La loi pénitentiaire peut être améliorée", http://www.interieur.gouv.fr/sections/a_la_une/toute_l_actualite/securite-interieure/brice-hortefeux-invite-questions-d-info/view. Viewed on 28 March 2011.

107   "Policiers condamnés: Hortefeux critique un jugement "disproportionné"", *Nouvelobs. com*, 11 December 2010,http://tempsreel.nouvelobs.com/actualite/societe/20101211. OBS4523/policiers-condamnes-hortefeux-critique-un-jugement-disproportionne.html. Viewed 28 March 2011.

108   For a reaction to these views and this conviction, see Michel Tubiana, Honorary President of the Human Rights League, "La forfaiture ou le mépris répété des lois les plus intimes de la République", *Le Monde*, 20 December 2010.

Political leaders who, like Brice Hortefeux, wished to represent an unweakened hard line against crime were compelled to criticize a law their own government had been promoting only a few months earlier.

Recidivism risks

Thus flow management comes into tension with anti-recidivism objectives. This tension increases every time a crime is committed by a person with a previous conviction. To criticize the penitentiary law's measures, UMP deputy Christian Vanneste cited the example of repeat offender Guy Georges[109]. Patrick Braouezec responded that it was "very easy to use the supreme and quite exceptional example of Guy Georges" and that, "aside from that exception, there are hundreds, thousands of people who were able to benefit from sentence adjustments and—perhaps thanks to this and to not having passed through prison where they could have made new contacts, as we know they do—were able to understand certain things and get back onto the 'straight and narrow path'"[110]. Christian Vanneste reckoned that "even a single death is one death too many!"[111].

The predominance of the question of recidivism was illustrated by the penal law debate that immediately followed the passing of the penitentiary law. Even though it would need to be verified quantitatively, this debate probably received more media attention than the penitentiary law debate, which had been awaited for almost ten years[112]. On 28 September 2009, a woman was abducted in Essonne. She was found dead a few days later. It soon emerged that the main murder suspect was a man with a previous conviction. The drama quickly took on a political dimension when senior government officials intervened. On October 1st, Nicolas Sarkozy asked Brice

---

109 A serial killer who received a life sentence in 2001 for seven poisoning murders.
110 Patrick Braouezec, National Assembly, 17 September 2009.
111 Christian Vanneste, National Assembly, 17 September 2009.
112 As an example of the analysis of press stances on a tragic news item, specifically the Buffet and Bontems affair (sentenced to death and executed in 1972 after an escape attempt involving a hostages that ended with the murder of the hostages) see Pierre Lascoumes, Ghislaine Moreau-Capdevielle (1976).

Hortefeux to study ways of expanding the monitoring of newly released prisoners, to reduce the risk of recidivism[113], possibly by means of legislative amendments. Moreover, "the president indicated that the anti-recidivism bill that was presented at a cabinet meeting last November would be considered by Parliament 'as a matter of priority' before the end of October"[114]. The AFP reported that the president was exhuming "a bill designed specifically to bolster the 'security surveillance' of released prisoners, which had been shelved for nearly a year"[115].

From that moment, the debate centred on the nature of amendments to be made to legislation and the question of so-called "chemical castration", that is, the possibility of imposing a hormonal treatment[116]. On 16 October, Nicolas Sarkozy confirmed that he favoured the use of "chemical castration" as a release condition for sexual offenders. The use of physical castration was once mentioned by Michèle Alliot-Marie[117]. In an interview in *le Figaro*, she said: "For the moment, physical castration is prohibited in France, but it is used elsewhere. I think it merits consideration, and today the question of physical castration can be raised and debated, including in Parliament"[118].

The Minister ultimately abandoned this argument, but the anti-recidivism bill was urgently tabled in Parliament. It was examined by a committee at the beginning of November, then passed by the National Assembly on 24 November 2009. Majority deputies toughened the government's text. The law provided for an expansion of security surveillance and the reimprisonment of released convicts who refused chemical castration in the context of a treatment injunction. However, the Assembly rejected amendments proposing sentence reduc-

---

113   "Sarkozy: surveiller davantage les condamnés ayant purgé leur peine (Elysée)", *AFP*, 1 October 2009.

114   *Ibid.*

115   "Sarkozy réactive le thème de la lutte contre la récidive pénale", *AFP,* 10 October 2009.

116   "Affaire Hodeau: MAM veut renforcer les mesures de castration chimique", *AFP*, 1 October 2009.

117   "Castration physique: 'la question peut être débattue' (Alliot-Marie)", *AFP*, 22 October 2009.

118   Michèle Alliot-Marie, "Une loi pour la castration chimique avant la fin de l'année", *Le Figaro,* 23 October 2009.

tions and a requirement to inform mayors when convicted sexual offenders moved to their cities[119]. In addition to left-wing parties and human rights organizations, the *Syndicat de la Magistrature* (the Union of the Magistracy), the *Syndicat des avocats de France* (the Lawyers' Union of France) and the SNEPAP-FSU[120] condemned the bill, stressing that reforms had been repeated in the area of anti-recidivism, that they had been toughened and represented an infringement of liberty, and that the adopted measures were ineffective. The bill was passed by the Senate, with changes relating to the minimum sentence length qualifying convicts for an end-of-sentence placement under judicial surveillance or socio-judicial tracking. Having been reduced from fifteen to ten years in the National Assembly, it was set back to fifteen years by the Senate, where the concession had been won in a joint committee[121]. The bill was finally passed on 25 February 2010[122].

The variations in political discourse illustrate the current complexities involved in dealing with sentence adjustments. Having been promised by the law—admittedly with reservations—they are virulently attacked whenever a case of criminal recidivism occurs. The law is then changed to make it more difficult to approve adjustments and make it easier to reimprison or to impose other forms of confinement (like secure detention) on people who have served their sentence but have failed to meet their obligations. These changes follow a trend towards turning the penal system into a risk and dangerousness management system, as symbolically represented by the February 2008 security detention law that we analyse in the next chapter.

---

119 "L'Assemblée vote le projet de loi récidive après l'avoir durci", *AFP*, 24 November 2009.

120 *Le Syndicat National de l'Ensemble des Personnels de l'Administration Pénitentiaire - Fédération Syndicale Unitaire* (The National Union of All Penitentiary Administration Personnel - the United Union Federation).

121 Jean-René Lecerf, Senate, 25 February 2010.

122 Law no. 2010-242 of 10 March 2010 to reduce the risk of criminal recidivism, containing various penal procedure clauses. http://www.assemblee-nationale.fr/13/dossiers/recidive_criminelle.asp.

CHAPTER 5
Treat, Evaluate... Imprison

I n Philip K. Dick's science fiction short story *The Minority Report*, special forces of the Precrime Agency have cut felonies "by ninety-nine and decimal point eight percent". By recording the prophecies of three "precogs" (precognitive mutants capable of seeing crimes that will be committed in the near future), these forces are able to intervene a week before the anticipated offence to prevent it; then they charge the virtual offender with the crime he would have committed and place the person they prevented from doing harm in a "detention camp for would-be criminals". *The Minority Report* describes the fantasy of France's justice system. This fiction powerfully illustrates the extent to which the demand for the neutralization of high-risk populations shifts the very terms of the debate on the justice system, and how it disconnects the punishment from the act.[123]

Three discursive reasons are advanced to justify new forms of prisoner classification: the need for differential adaptation to dangerousness, the need to take charge of, and treat, people who are ill and increasingly abnormal, and the need to assess the risk of post-release recidivism. These three reasons correspond to three factors affecting the transformation of the penal and penitentiary field. The first, as we have seen, is the characterization of differential regimes as central to reform. But, in order to make this desire for classification acceptable, its defenders must present scientific evidence that justifies its

---

123   On "precrime society", see Lucia Zedner (2007).

evaluations as a new way of managing prisoner categories, and as a form of post-release recidivism prevention. This leads to the second factor, the desire to remove barriers separating prison's penitentiary and medical domains, to lay the foundations for multidisciplinary prisoner assessments. The third is a legal innovation concurrent with the development of the penitentiary law, consisting in a law allowing those who have finished serving their full sentences to be held indefinitely in the name of secure detention. This law was presented as being intended for a very small minority of prisoners, but it introduced into the public debate the idea that reaching the end of a sentence did not necessarily mean being released. These questions indicate points of fundamental confrontation between rights and new penalty controls: classification versus equality of rights, information sharing versus the right to healthcare, risk evaluation versus the right to freedom and, more broadly, the rights guaranteed by the determination of the length of sentences.

Treatment

One way to legitimize these classifications is to base them on the notion of treatment, specifically psychiatric treatment. Historian Marc Renneville (2004) formulated a hypothesis at the end of his two-century study on the relationship between crime and madness: what if the incarceration of people who have been declared mentally ill had quietly become one of the established uses of prison, despite being ceaselessly denounced and discredited as a technique for rectifying deviant behaviour? Behind this question, several issues become entangled: that of the nature of the partial, gradual redistribution of psychiatric confinement towards prison confinement; that of the effect this redistribution has on sufferers' confinement conditions, either in prison or in hospitals; that, finally, of the transformation of the very meaning of psychiatric practice as it grapples with the constraints of prison operations[124].

---

124   For a discussion of these processes in the American conext, See Rhodes (1991), Rhodes (2004).

One factor often cited to explain the fact that psychiatric confinement is being partially redistributed to prisons is the drop, over the past twenty years, in the number cases being dismissed due to exemption from criminal responsibility, the result of a political and psychiatric drive to "empower the mentally ill". Yet after intense debate over how this number is evolving, it seems certain that the trend is a downward one (212 cases dismissed due to exemption from criminal responsibility in 2005, compared with 340 in 1995 and 444 in 1987). But it started with a rate that has always been low, and it cannot alone explain the broader trend. In addition to the increased scarcity of cases of exemption from criminal responsibility, there is broader institutional restructuring in progress. On the one hand, the opening of asylums as part of the psychiatric hospital deinstitutionalization trend that began in the 1970s, as well as the development of sector psychiatry[125], help explain the drop in the number of beds available: from over 120,000 hospital beds in 1970 to 40,000 in 2005. Psychiatric hospitals in particular have very limited resources for accommodating patients considered dangerous. On the other hand, the ordinary justice train is being accelerated by means of the summary trial procedure[126], which is most often applied to perpetrators of visible crimes, in the street, who are in situations of social marginality. Studies have shown that a significant number of people with untreated psychiatric illnesses who are socially isolated follow a path of exclusion that passes through prison or jail and ends in the street (even in the morgue; some psychiatrists linked the prevalence of schizophrenia among the homeless to the number of people who die of the cold in winter). When these people are arrested and then sent

---

125 Sector psychiatry refers to the administrative organization managing mental illness and the division of mental healthcare structures. Presented as a break with "hospital centrism", the sector psychiatry policy encouraged, from the beginning of the 1970s, the development of "extramural" care, and a wider distribution of psychiatric services in the city. This distribution was underpinned by the idea, in embryo since the end of the Second World War, that treatment must be moved, to bring it closer to where the patients live.

126 A procedure that enables a very quick judgement for offenders caught in the act. See Christin and Bastard (2008), Mouhanna and Ackermann (2005).

into a high-speed justice system, there is little chance that their psychiatric disorders will be recognized and treated. A petition by psychiatrists summed up the situation:

> "General psychiatric services are having major problems caring for difficult and violent patients (fewer beds, less doctors, decreased workforce). Lacking suitable care structures, hospitals leave these individuals on the streets until their symptoms turn them to crime and land them in prison. Prisons or jails then become the last institution able to accommodate them. They are replacing asylums and becoming the place to which psychiatric cases are relegated"[127].

Conversely, the idleness of incarceration is conducive to decompensation, and when these cases are directed to prison psychiatrists, it is another chance for them to deplore the justice system's inability to recognize people's need for treatment before sending them to prison.

Other mechanisms intensify the process at work. Since 1994, the Penal Code has provided that, midway between full responsibility and total exemption from responsibility (lack of discernment at the moment of the alleged offence) people can be tried and convicted if their responsibility has been deemed "attenuated" (distorted discernment). This clause was designed to reduce penalties by recognizing partial responsibility. But the dismal irony of this mechanism is that in practice, having been found guilty, insane and dangerous, people whose distorted discernment has been recognized often receive heavier sentences. They are reduced to drifting between ordinary detention quarters, the scarce psychiatric hospitalization places available in

---

127 Gérard Dubret, Luc Massardier and Philippe Carrière, "Hôpitaux- prisons: le remède sera pire que le mal", a petition against the creation of Specially Equipped Hospital Wards [*Unités hospitalières spécialement aménagées* (UHSA)], 2007. The petition called for more Wards for Difficult Patients [*Unités pour malades difficiles* (UMD)], in order to be able to treat difficult patients in advance of incarceration, to avoid this. It also condemned the segregative and stigmatizing UHSA strategy. http://www.prison.eu.org/article.php3?id_article=9661. Viewed on 28 March 2011.

detention, disciplinary wings, solitary confinement, and compulsory hospitalization, which has increased fifteenfold in the space of ten years. Even once they have completed the period of unconditional detention during which sentence adjustments cannot be requested, they have very limited access to these, which require a rehabilitation plan to be presented that includes housing and employment.

Another pernicious effect was denounced in a consensus conference report: that more treatment in prisons meant more incarceration for the mentally ill.

"Some assessments establishing a distortion of discernment also conclude that care needs to be provided by the regional medical and psychological service (RMPS), giving rise to the belief that these RMPSs, in spite of being located in prisons, can become treatment centres in their own right, and not simply a place 'where treatment is offered'. This confusion can exacerbate the apprehension of healthcare staff, who are bitterly aware that their presence in prisons tends to legitimize the repression of the mentally ill in the justice system."

In 2009, this knock-on effect was further reinforced by the creation of Specially Equiped Hospital Wards (UHSA). The Correctional service effectively expanded the prison infrastructure by establishing secure treatment facilities within hospitals, exclusively for the hospitalization of prisoners with psychiatric disorders. Many psychiatrists viewed the creation of UHSAs as a humanitarian emergency measure that responded to the deleterious conditions of the mentally ill in prison (isolation, excessive disciplinary punishment, suicidality, drastic decompensation). But others—even some of the same—feared that these very facilities would lead to greater acceptance of the incarceration of the mentally ill. As psychiatrist Gérard Dubret explained, "developing psychiatric hospitalization facilities within the penitentiary system that are able to treat the most serious pathologies, without taking advance steps to remedy the influx into prison of people with mental illnesses, definitely raises the risk of increasing this tendency". "Unfortunately", he continues, "offering more psychiatric care in prison also means increasing the risk that courts will hand more prison sentences to people with mental illnesses, since incarceration would be accompanied by psychiatric treatment, even for the most serious pathologies" (Dubret 2005).

The attention that the question of medical confidentiality has received from the Minister of Justice can be understood at the conjunction of the tendency to incarcerate people with psychiatric disorders, the tendency to liken psychiatric disorders to dangerousness, and the tendency to liken imprisonment to treatment. This rhetorical and practical continuity does not square with the fundamental prison healthcare reform passed in 1994. It effectively transferred the care of prisoners to public hospitals. Prison medicine was therefore subject to the same deontological rules as ordinary medicine. The reform put an end to the long tradition of "penitentiary medicine", a term that designated substandard care integrated into the prison disciplinary system. In the early 1970s, a young doctor from Paris's La Santé jail published a book in which he recounted that, when he arrived, the director had instructed him to expose "fakers" who consulted him without reason. Prisoners he identified were punished (Dayant 1972). He saw a hunger striker being weighed and teased ("you should shave, it distorts the results") (Dayant 1972, 60). The 1994 law was passed to put an end to this situation (Lechien, 2001, Farges, 2007).

By defining the role of prison medical services in this way, the reform distanced them from two roles that the courts and the Correctional Service increasingly needed: participation in the maintenance of prison order though information sharing and risk evaluation, and the assessment of dangerousness when there was the prospect of release. The shift to a strict focus on treatment did not proceed without conflict. Doctors were given the power to refuse to apply a disciplinary penalty on health grounds, specifically when they found contraindications to placement in disciplinary wings. This conflict between professionals operating according to different rules represented in itself a weakening of the Correctional Service's power.

This is why since 2007, the Minister of Justice has been leading a drive to revoke what she considers an overly strict separation between medical staff and those responsible for prison security. It is in this context that one should understand attacks against medical confidentiality and efforts to replace it with a "shared secret" policy. According to Rachida Dati, this new policy would "enable the Correctional Service to benefit from a strictly controlled exchange of information from prisoners' medical files in order to improve their care and improve security"[128]. An article that was slipped into the 2008 law provides that: "As soon as there is a serious risk to people's security [...], [medical staff working within prisons] having knowledge of this risk are required to inform the prison director as soon as possible, by giving him—respecting clauses relative to medical confidentiality—information that can be used for the implementation of protective measures"[129]. Dati later defended this clause:

"The Correctional Service has no access to prisoners' criminal files; it only knows the conviction and is unaware of all medical aspects. This is what led to the drama that occurred at the Rouen jail, where a prisoner committed acts of cannibalism against his fellow prisoner. It was only later that we became aware that this person presented this kind of psychiatric disorder. Also, to prevent these events from reoccurring, we wanted [...] to take information sharing further, by authorizing the Correctional Service to have cognizance of elements not of a medical nature, but relating to security. These elements are given to

---

128   Rachida Dati, *Le Parisien*, 5 October 2007.
129   Law of 25 February 2008 relating to secure detention and the declaration of exemption from criminal responsibility on account of mental illness, article 8.

prison staff by medical staff in order to protect not only the prisoner and his fellow prisoners, but also prison staff. Medical confidentiality for consultations with nurses, psychologists and doctors is therefore totally preserved, limited only by security. [...] The notion of medical confidentiality must be considered pragmatically, because the lives of penitentiary and medical staff must not be endangered"[130].

A depiction such as this, highlighting a dreadful prison crime to defend changing the role of doctors[131], obviously excludes any consideration of the reasons for the perpetrator's very presence in prison. In this case, the desire to neutralize the threat presented by people considered insane and dangerous takes efforts to legitimize confinement to the limit.

Evaluating, imprisoning

Significantly, this clause on medical confidentiality in prison represented the creation of a major penal reform: the establishment of the possibility of indefinite post-sentence imprisonment, called secure detention. At the end of February 2008, the law concerning secure detention and the declaration of exclusion from criminal responsibility due to mental illness took effect. Now prisoners serving sentences of fifteen years or more for crimes committed against a minor (murder or manslaughter, torture or barbarous acts, rape, kidnapping or false imprisonment) or crimes committed against an adult (murder and/or manslaughter, torture or aggravated barbarous acts, aggravated rape, aggravated kidnapping or false imprisonment) could, at the end of their sentence, be placed under secure detention for one year, renewable indefinitely. The Constitutional Council validated the law, deeming that this confinement was not a penalty (something that would have been contrary

130   Rachida Dati, Senate, 5 March 2009.
131   "Après autopsie du détenu tué à Rouen, l'acte de cannibalisme semble établi", *Libération*, 6 January 2007.

to the principle that penalties must have a sound legal basis) but paradoxically deeming that this confinement could not be retroactive (even though the *ex post facto* principle is a penalty principle). Furthermore, the Constitutional Council accepted retroactivity for "secure surveillance", which can involve—without any time limit—being placed under electronic surveillance and being required to meet a number of obligations. Anyone who contravened these obligations would, this time, be liable to security detention, the *ex post facto* principle having been set aside in this scenario as well.

This measure provided the experts consulted at the end of the sentence with the power to keep prisoners in detention. Retention can be ordered if a "particular dangerousness" has been observed in the prisoner. Yet those who promoted this reform were well aware of the insubstantiality of such a diagnosis. According to a report by senior judge François Burgelin, who was the first to propose establishing security detention in 2005, "international studies on the recidivism of criminals with mental disorders and perpetrators of sexual offences have revealed that the dangerousness of many individuals was either overestimated or underestimated", the former—wrongly considered dangerous—being "of the order of 60-85%" (Burgelin 2005). In other words, the predictions tend to judge people to be more "dangerous" than they are, since saying someone presents "no risk" is a prognosis that is very... risky, even if cases of recidivism relating to the most serious offences concern only a very small minority of convicted persons. This is why designating people as presenting an "extremely high" risk does not make sense, further demonstrating the perverse rationale of selective incapacitation (Mathiesen 1998). The aim of secure detention is to release prisoners only when they present no risk whatsoever. Who would authorize the release of someone whose recidivism risk was considered "high" or "medium"? What would happen if someone were released and then were to reoffend because his risk was not "extremely high"?

It is true that the original bill only concerned perpetrators of crimes against minors under the age of 15. But the National Assembly completely changed this legal limit. The law was placed on the parliamentary agenda after a repeat offender sexually assaulted a minor. An amendment was tabled to extend the use of secure detention to include perpetrators of certain crimes against adults. The result of this fundamental transformation of the law was that MPs passed the bill without having any solid figures on the number of people who would be affected. International comparisons on the matter show that a secure detention logic based on risk prediction is inflationary. In Holland (cited as an example in the bill) in 2006, secure confinement "concerns 1,400 people, of which some sixty, currently accommodated in a long-term facility, will probably never be released". Moreover, "if current tendencies continue, the number of people placed in secure confinement could rise to 2,500 by 2010".

This rationale eliminates any possibility of a link to treatment, as evinced by empirical studies conducted in other countries using similar systems, such as "civil commitment" in the United States, or in Germany (another example cited in the bill), where a parliamentary report observed that: "while the law requires specific and individualized treatment for every person affected by the security measure, in practice it seems almost impossible to motivate people and interest them in a life in society when its prospects seem so hypothetical"[132]. So it would be better to call indefinite security detention in prisons a "life sentence for people who are not allowed to receive this sentence under the Penal Code". Initial sentence length would be nothing more than the equivalent of the minimum term of a life sentence, that is, the period during which no application for parole can be requested.

These changes rest upon a rationale whose strength lies in its very simplicity, as a right-wing political leader demonstrated during discussions on secure detention retroactivity: "I'll leave it up to the French people to make up their minds about the Socialist Party, which clearly sides with murderers, forgetting all of the victims. It is irrespon-

132   Jean-René Lecerf, *Rapport sur le Projet de loi relatif à la rétention de sûreté et à la déclaration d'irresponsabilité pénale pour cause de trouble mental*, Senate, 23 January 2008.

sible to play with the safety of the French people [...] raising the question of the retroactivity of the law for convicted murderers and child rapists is primarily the desire to ensure the safety of the French people [...] It is about applying the precautionary principle"[133]. Prison reform bills incorporate this paradigm by linking the demand for caution to the practice of evaluating and classifying prisoners, which relies on a new system of information sharing between doctors and those responsible for security. A new assessment that combined penitentiary and medical expertise would be used to divide up prisoners upon their arrival, in order to prevent threats to prison safety and, in the most serious cases, to determine the possibility of release.

In spite of the medical treatment prisoners may be (irregularly) offered, a judgement by the European Court of Human Rights confirmed the tragic nature of life in the prison system. On 11 July 2006, it condemned France for having kept a prisoner suffering from psychiatric disorders in confinement for several years without appropriate medical supervision. This criticism very precisely highlighted the kind of problem that will affect post-sentence holding centres in the future: a person had finished serving a long sentence, but his release was delayed due to psychiatric disorders. These worsened significantly in prison, to the point that releasing him seemed unthinkable. Since a sentence adjustment was not possible and there was no external accommodation available, the courts had sentenced this person to a gradual deterioration of his health in prison, a result that was later invoked to decline his release. Tomorrow, the same law could pursue its program of non-treatment by means of potentially permanent secure detention. As former Minister of Justice (1981-1986) Robert Badinter (Socialist

---

133   "Nadine Morano accuse le PS de 'se ranger' du côté des assassins", 13 June 2008. http://tempsreel.nouvelobs.com/article/20080224.OBS1994/nadine-morano-accuse-le-ps-de-se-ranger-du-cote-des-assassins.html. Viewed on 28 March 2011. A judgement standard whose meaning and scope are established in practice, the general notion of the precautionary principle was first developed in the context of the environment, then health (Lascoumes, 1997). It suggests that the absence of certainties, taking account of current scientific and technical knowledge, should not delay the adoption of effective measures aiming to prevent a risk of serious and irreversible damage.

Party) wrote, "the word that comes to mind to characterize them is that of Victor Hugo: '*misérables*'. These are what our psychiatrized justice system will produce tomorrow in our prisons"[134].

The extended confinement and deteriorating health of mentally ill prisoners are symptomatic of how the therapeutic apparatus is being stifled by a penal system built around control and maximum security. Here we concur with Bastien Quirion. At the end of his analysis of the transformation of a modern medical treatment system, he concluded that in terms of understanding the innovation or inertia of medical treatment resources on the whole, the sociopolitical context overdetermined knowledge and techniques (Quirion 2007). In other words, the contemporary objectives of the penal system overshadow and undermine psychiatric knowledge, psychiatric techniques, and the therapeutic relationship itself. People with mental illnesses who have committed serious offences are sent to prison in full cognizance of their pathology, in order to avoid any possibility of escape. They are given very long sentences to delay their release. They do not receive treatment when compulsory hospitalization is ordered because maximum security conditions are imposed upon them. Tomorrow, their incarceration might still be restricted by the legal duration of the sentence, but at the end of this, they will go to holding centres that will be no better able to provide treatment.

---

134   Robert Badinter, "La prison après la peine", *Le Monde*, 27 November 2007.

CHAPTER 6
Walled Up Alive

"We, who have been walled up alive for life at the highest security prison in France (...) call for the death penalty to be reinstated for us. Enough hypocrisy! Since in reality we have been doomed to a life sentence, with no genuine prospect of release at the end of our minimum term, we much prefer to get it over with, instead of dying a slow death with no hope for tomorrow, after well over twenty years of absolute misery. Unlike other European countries, behind the grey walls of its disgraceful prisons, the 'Republic of Enlightenment and Liberty' of 2006 is quietly torturing and annihilating us, apparently in an entirely lawful manner, 'in the name of the French people'. [...] What is the point of the minimum terms imposed upon us if once this time has been duly served, we have no hope of regaining freedom? [...] After terms of this length, survivors leave senile and utterly defeated at best. Under these circumstances, who can really be socially rehabilitated? In fact, out of all of the alternatives, does nothing better remain than to seek a quicker freedom through death, as in the time before 1981? And to get us resigned to the fate of being buried alive, in recent years we have been given more walls, watchtowers, steel bars and many other constraints. [...]. And since a so-called 'democratic' society should not be allowed to play around like this with a penal policy that aims to lengthen sentences indefinitely depending on the situation, the individual or particular needs: given the choice, instead of a slow, scheduled death, we ask the government of France, the voice of human rights and liberties, to instantly re-establish the real death penalty for all of us."

This petition, dated 16 January 2006, was a political event[135]. Signed by ten prisoners serving long sentences at Clairvaux prison, it was smuggled out and then widely reported in the media. A "we" was taking shape and speaking where before there had been nothing but silence or noise (Rancière 1995, 51-53). Through a unique subjectification process, prisoners who were "walled up alive" revealed the wrong to which they had been subjected. They asserted their distance from the various monstrous images used to describe perpetrators of serious crime, and from the kind of prison slang that nicknamed prisoners "*Longue Peine*[136]". More than anything else, they undermined all of the obvious facts most often associated with the abolition of the death penalty. They denounced a change in how the power to punish was exercised. The progressive nature of the change was highly illusory: "instead of throwing the bloody flesh of the slashed convict to the Minotaur, the creature was being offered braised lives, so to speak" (Perrault 2001, 54). The petitioners provided an opportunity to reconsider a question formulated in the 1970s by Pierre Goldman in *Souvenirs obscurs d'un juif polonais né en France*[137]. Goldman was an extreme left-wing militant incarcerated for a fatal robbery he denied having committed, and his trial sparked major demonstrations. He spent a few years in prison before being murdered. He did not want to chronicle his prison years in his book, but it contained a long text in italics that appeared

---

135 For example, the appeal made the front page of the daily newspaper *Libération* on 30 January 2006.
136 Literally "long sentence".
137 Literally: *Obscure Memories of a Polish Jew Born in France* (unpublished in English).

to have been written all in one go. The final question in the text is the one raised by the petitioners. A friend of Pierre Goldman, whom he sees the day and evening before his trial verdict, escapes the death penalty still in force, but: "can one say: my dear Pierre I got a life sentence, what a slight improvement (what luck?)" (Goldman 1975, 116).

The process of subjectifying prisoners who are "walled up alive" is part of the exacerbation of the prison system's historical contradictions. This is why the Clairvaux petition provides a unique opportunity to understand one of them: the fact that the spectre of true life sentences should reappear in an institution that claims to be granting more rights to the men and women it keeps behind bars.

Granting rights, walling up

In October 2006, the French government declared that it was taking ownership of the European Prison Rules passed by the Committee of Ministers of the Council of Europe in January of the same year. The government acknowledged the validity of a list of recommendations aiming to bring European prisons in line with the requirements of the European Convention on Human Rights, as interpreted by the European Court of Human Rights. This proclamation followed a number of declarations by Ministers about the need to subject prisons to the rule of law. But the Minister of Justice initially excluded from national application the section of these European standards that guaranteed prisoners' right to collective expression on life in detention—keeping any future statements like that of the "Clairvaux Ten[138]" in secrecy. Specifically, rule 50 states that "subject to the needs of good order, safety and security, prisoners shall be allowed to discuss matters relating to the general conditions of imprisonment and shall be encouraged to communicate

---

138   These potentialities are all the stronger in that this legislative framework is supported by guard training and sensitization, and that it is subject to rigorous internal and external oversight. See Norman Bishop (2006), http://champpenal.revues.org/document485. html. On the roles of prisoner committees in the regulation of behaviour in Canadian penitentiaries, see Gilles Chantraine (2009a).

with the prison authorities about these matters". Of course, suspending the right to expression for security reasons immediately limits its reach. But countries such as Belgium, Denmark, Finland, Germany, the Netherlands, Spain and Sweden, which to varying degrees have legislation relating to prisoner participation in the general management of prisons (particularly in the form of "prisoner consultative committees"), at least make it possible to understand the potential of these forums and other opportunities to discuss the conflicts the institution engenders. Without them, these conflicts have no other outlet than violence (against others or against oneself) and penalties.

The minister did not say a word about the standards promoted by the Council of Europe, which asked member states to ensure that prisoners serving long sentences have *realistic* prospects of release and that they are given the opportunity to prepare for this in prison. In particular, "in order to reduce the harmful effects of imprisonment and to promote the resettlement of prisoners under conditions that seek to guarantee safety of the outside community," the Council of Europe considers that "the law should make parole available to all sentenced prisoners, including life-sentence prisoners"[139]. If the sentence includes a term during which a sentence adjustment is not possible, it recommends that "the minimum or fixed period should not be so long that the purpose of parole cannot be achieved". And, as for the approval process, the Council considers that "the criteria that prisoners have to fulfil in order to be granted parole should be clear and explicit" and that these criteria "should be applied so as to grant parole to all prisoners who are considered as meeting the minimum level of safeguards for becoming law-abiding citizens. It should be incumbent on the authorities to show that a prisoner has not fulfilled the criteria."

By contrast, the "walled up" petitioners exposed three contemporary tendencies in French penal policy. First, the

---

139   Council of Europe, *Recommendation concerning the management of life-sentenced and other long-term prisoners*, 2003, in Council of Europe (2009).

prolongation of long sentences, specifically by granting parole less often. In 1977, the journal *Actes*, founded by law researchers and practitioners, noted that, according to 1975 statistics, 70% of prisoners in detention centres left on parole; the figure was 65% in prisons. The journal considered this a good measure and deemed that it was still being "granted meagrely" (Collectif 1997). The editors were unaware that they were writing at the beginning of a period when this measure would be ever more meagrely granted. As the CNCDH observed, "parole rates have been halved in thirty years. The number of approvals compared with the number of eligible prisoners descended from 29.3% in 1973 to 15% in 1999". According to the commission, the "principal cause of the decline in the granting of parole [is] pressure placed on judges, which in large part explains why 87% of prisoners released on parole are serving sentences under 5 years. For long sentences, that is, for more serious offences, there is a greater risk of drawing wide disapproval, particularly in cases of recidivism by paroled prisoners." (CNCDH 2007b).

A second tendency: to conceive of release in terms of risk—zero risk for the most serious offences. This legislative trend indicates that penal policy is focusing its most repressive efforts on particular offence categories, foremost among which are sexual offences, especially those whose victims are children. To understand this change, one must connect the push to recognize women's and children's right (and efforts to criminalize attacks against them) with the emergence of a risk reduction approach to penal policy. In this sense, what must be linked is a decade-long trend towards recognizing victims and their rights, a risk reduction approach, and a risk reduction policy line that promotes zero risk so that it can incorporate long sentences. The grisly nature of sexual crime is coupled with a claim that zero risk is the only possible paradigm. Here the point is not so much to change people, but rather to adopt measures that eliminate them from society and/or subject them to perpetual monitoring, rationalized by the intolerable character of certain crimes.

Finally, at the intersection of these two tendencies, is the depoliticization of the collective demand for freedom, a demand that has been stifled by the individual dangerousness prognosis established by experts. The notion of dangerousness thus becomes a powerful lever for individualizing the prison issue. These three tendencies, entrenched through the increasingly long terms actually being served by life sentence prisoners, paved the way for secure detention, recommended in a so-called "Health/Justice" report in 2005 (Burgelin 2005) and then in a Senate report[140]. The subjectification of the walled-up petitioners reflected this particular tension between rights promotion and the arbitrariness of contemporary crime control. It is all the more salient in that, as the petitioners pointed out, the infiniteness of their sentences— the arbitrariness of their release date—is coupled with the priority given to maximum security in everyday prison life[141]. This increasing emphasis on security, which is just as arbitrary, becomes a supplementary object of struggle.

Up until 2002, in prisons that, like Clairvaux, housed long-sentence prisoners and those considered most troublesome, prisoners benefitted from one form of tolerance: cell doors remained open during the day, allowing them to circulate within their own wing. In 2002 Dominique Perben decided to gradually withdraw this tolerance. The prisoners at Clairvaux, who were the first affected, reacted by setting fire to their workshops. The policy was then implemented at other prisons, not without tension. Collectives stood up for the rebels ("Long live the mutineers!"). The European Committee for the Prevention of Torture (CPT), visiting France the following year, asked the authorities to reverse their decision (CPT 2004a), as did a minority guards' union (the CGT Pénitentiaire[142]), which considered the closed-door regime to be reminiscent of the notorious High Security

---

140　"Les délinquants dangereux atteints de troubles psychiatriques: comment concilier la protection de la société et une meilleure prise en charge médicale ?", an information report by senators Philippe Goujon and Charles Gautier, June 2006. On secure detention, see chapter 5.

141　For an ethnography of the day-to-day life in French prisons, see (Le Caisne 2000). On American maximum-security prisons, see (Rhodes 2004); (Jeffrey 2007).

142　Literally: The General Confederation of Work.

Wings[143]. The Minister remained obstinate, replying sharply that the CPT could do whatever it wanted (CPT 2004b).

In November 2003, two prisoners at the Moulins-Yzeure prison took a guard hostage in their workshop. They stayed there for a few hours in the company of other prisoners. No violence occurred; the two prisoners demanded "respect", activities, and the return of the "doors-open" regime. Not long before, at the time when the decision was made to close the doors, Correctional Service established Regional Response and Security Teams (ERIS[144]) made up of elite members of the security staff who, following the example of response teams in the police (GIPN) and the Gendarmerie (GIGN), had received special training to perform masked interventions. On 24 November, they were called to the workshop, as were members of the Gendarmerie. Satisfied that they had "succeeded in drawing attention to their problem", the hostage-takers surrendered and calmly freed everyone. That evening, the Minister warmly congratulated the ERIS for the success of their first intervention. The local prosecutor, who rushed to the scene, wrote to his superiors that everything had gone splendidly.

However, a few months later, requested by the hostage-takers through an MP, the National Commission on Ethics and Security (CNDS) launched an inquiry into the conditions under which the hostage-taking had ended (CNDS 2005). The statements they collected on site were contradictory and manifestly untrue. The prison guards, the ERIS and the Gendarmerie accused each other of violence. According to the commission, the prisoners were beaten as they were taken to the disciplinary wing (DW). They were then stripped with the help of a utility knife as a riot shield was pressed against their heads. Then they were forced to spend their first night in the DW half naked, without sheets or toilet paper. The CNDS believed that it was "very likely that guards from Moulins—belonging to the local intervention group, with

---

143   On High-Security Wings and how the Correctional Service analyzed their history, see chapter 3.

144   Équipes régionales d'intervention et de sécurité.

is essentially composed of Moulins officers—intervened, in masks, into the workshop with great violence, both in retaliation for having taken their colleagues hostage and as part of a destructive atmosphere of 'competition' with their colleagues in the newly formed ERISs". The CNDS found that "the prisoners were returned to the disciplinary wing under particularly grave and disgraceful conditions, which were violent and in violation of their human dignity". In the commission's view, "many of the officers from the prison present here are entirely responsible for the events that resulted in indefensible violence". It clearly emerged that the hostage-takers had been beaten by members of the different groups that had attended, in full view of the prison hierarchy, which had kept silent. The commission requested disciplinary penalties. The director was transferred. The prisoners responsible for the hostage-taking had already been tried and handed new four-year sentences[145].

Two conflicting penal modernities

These stories of revolts, hostage-taking and retaliatory physical violence resemble many others that adorn the history of the Correctional Service's handling of acts of insubordination. But they are also perfectly modern. The hostage-taking took place in a recently constructed prison, the most secure in Europe, specially dedicated to the confinement of long-sentence prisoners. It did not involve "old style" prison guards, who fix problems with their fists (Carlier 1996), but a newly created group. It was not revealed secretly, through information leaked in order to denounce the silence, but by an official commission, established in 2000.

The story illustrates the ambivalence of the shifting relationship between the prison institution, the rights of prisoners, and violence. This violence goes against the purported code of ethics. And it is rooted in the relationship between prisoners without hope on the one hand, wasting

---

145   Juse over six years later, the prison's director and head of detention were indicted for complicity in deliberate acts of violence.

away without any forum for negotiation, and masked guards on the other. At a time when the Correctional Service was incorporating monitoring bodies (largely against its will), it was providing some of these guards with an anonymity liable to inspire excesses and a feeling of impunity. For this reason, the European Committee for the Prevention of Torture asked the French government (unsuccessfully) to "prohibit the wearing of masks of any kind by members of the ERIS during their interventions" (CPT 2004a, CPT 2004b).

The decisions to close the doors and to establish a masked guard corps contradicted the recommendations of the Council of Europe, which stressed the need to limit the "desocializing effects" of incarceration, especially for people serving long sentences[146]. These recommendations are consistent with others concerning penal policy, which encourage member states to shorten detention time through parole. The consistency is not only intellectual, but directly concerns the management of life in detention. The security constraints required for a prisoner who has a realistic prospect of being released under correct conditions are much less than those needed for the imprisonment of people who have no forthcoming or predictable hope of release—all the more so if the zero-escapes objective is asserted as a priority. According to Sonja Snacken (1997), who drew up one of the few overviews of research into this question, for prisoners, long-term detention increases the risk of "institutionalization", in other words, the risk of becoming entirely dependent upon the institution. She identified other psychopathological effects, such as aggression against oneself (suicide, self-mutilation). Although institutionalization processes depend on each prison's unique organization (specifically, the degree of prisoner autonomy, how much they participate in orienting community life and the number of contacts they can maintain with the outside world), the length of detention itself is a key variable in the institutionalization process. This observation is

146   Council of Europe, *Recommendation concerning the management of life-sentenced and other long-term prisoners*, 2003, in Council of Europe (2009).

consistent with the results of two studies carried out in France highlighting the mechanisms linking violence to detention time. M. Guilloneau and A. Kensey showed that protracted detention and heavy sentences explain the increase in attacks against personnel over the past few years (Kensey et Guillonneau 1998). Also, A. Chauvenet, F. Orlic and C. Rostaing showed that detention time aggravated all of the problems of incarceration: "Over time, all of prison's constraints grow harder to accept, because they seem more and more intense. Touchiness, short-temperedness, aggression, anxiety, constant mood changes, being forced to grin and bear it all, the elimination of the real world and of all links with the outside world in favour of an imagination in which one has time to brood at one's leisure, turning in on oneself, paranoia, lack of activity, impotence, the waiting and dependence, all of these incarceration effects will worsen over time" (Chauvenet, Orlic and Rostaing 2008). And yet the existing penal policy assigns the Correctional Service the task of enforcing a mandate of strict containment. Under these conditions, directors highlight "tensions" and the majority guard unions demand extra security measures, specifically the construction of special prisons for people declared and classified as "dangerous".

Following a violent escape from the Moulins prison in early 2009, the Correctional Service announced it was establishing a working group on the management of long-sentence prisoners. The same work had already been done fifteen years earlier under similar circumstances (Inspection générale de l'administration et Inspection des services judiciaires 1993). Having been summoned in the aftermath of violent escapes, attempted escapes and revolts (particularly in the prisons in Moulins, Saint-Maur and Clairvaux), the Inspectorate General of the Correctional Service and the Inspectorate General of Judicial Services had considered the causes of these tragic events. They had concluded that "the fact that these prisoners, considering the length of their sentences, had no reasonable hope of release in the medium-term, nor any real fear of having their penalties increased, no doubt has something to do the violence of their attempts [at escape]". And yet, they observed, the number of prisoners being handed these sentences was increasing, and managing them was a "source of considerable challenges".

The 1993 report on long sentences set out a clear alternative: "either find mechanisms to correct the increase in the number and length of long sentences, or adapt the prisons to this new fact". It should come as no surprise which of these two alternatives was actually implemented. To take only the example of the harshest sentence, a 2005 survey of 151 people who initially received commuted death sentences or life sentences and were released between 1995-2005, showed that their average detention time—around twenty years—was "three years longer than that observed" during previous surveys. Among this group, "one in five prisoners (20.5%) had been incarcerated for over twenty-two years" whereas previously "these long detentions were rare" (only 1.6% of those released between 1961 and 1980). Moreover, a review of the files of prisoners serving life sentences on 1 May 2005 (562 people) gave a glimpse of the increase in this tendency: 23% of them had been convicted at least twenty years earlier, 17% at least thirty years earlier, of which 3% had served forty years or more (Kensey 2005).

As the 1993 report explained, "it is a fundamental safeguard for prison personnel that prisoners should have a hope of being released" (Inspection générale de l'administration et Inspection des services judiciaires 1993). Without this, the Correctional Service will increase the constraining and desocializing nature of security systems following every case of serious violence, creating what is known as a "supermax" in the United States, where people are locked up twenty-four hours a day without any possibility of contact with others, only able to walk between the walls of a tiny room, without any activities or work. As the director of Human Rights Watch's US program explained, these prisons find their rationalization in the fact that, in that country, "there are no more early releases [...], there are only increasingly strict detention regimes" (Fellner

2005). Supermax prisons are not specifically intended for people who have committed the most serious crimes, they are a component of the disciplinary system.

Since it is not possible to reward good behaviour with freedom, the Correctional Service rewards it by: a) not transferring the prisoner to a higher-security prison, or sparing him constant transfers to the four corners of France[147]; b) not placing the prisoner in isolation, a security measure that can last years and can do irreversible damage to the physical and mental health of the person concerned. This is what prompted the CNDS, in November 2008, to denounce the treatment of a prisoner who, after escaping in 1992, "was transferred some sixty times and placed in isolation for twelve and a half years"[148].

These kinds of disciplinary decisions are facing more and more legal challenges. In fact, since 1995, the number of so-called "internal" decisions—taken by the CS and not able to be challenged before an administrative tribunal—is on the decrease. Placement in disciplinary wings now takes place under the watchful eye of a judge. The Council of State, the highest administrative tribunal, in three General Assembly rulings on 14 December 2007, recognized the admissibility of appeals against downgrading decisions (eg. the withdrawal of employment), against a decision to transfer a prisoner from a prison to a jail, and finally against a decision to subject a prisoner to a so-called "security rotations regime", meaning constant transfers. This jurisprudential trend "showed the most life in 2008, when around ten rulings of the highest importance were made, either by the Administrative Court of Appeal or the Council of State" (de Suremain and Bérard 2009). But the CS fought tooth and nail against these jurisprudential developments. In a context such as this, the legal tug-of-war can assume insid-

---

147   These repeated transfers, known in France as "prison tourism", aim first and foremost to break the social links that the prisoner attempts to construct in prison in spite of everything. As a reduced form of "diesel therapy" (Niles 1999), these transfers aggravate the pains of imprisonment while eliminating every possibility of escape.

148   Alain Salles, "L'isolement d'un détenu pendant près de treize ans jugé 'inhumain'", *Le Monde*, 12 December 2008.

ious forms. For example, a 2006 decree on isolation, made necessary by a 2003 Council of State decision, placed long-term isolation under judicial oversight... but also authorized longer placements in isolation[149]. Similarly, within detention centres—penal establishments theoretically dedicated to "rehabilitation"—differential detention regimes were reintroduced, of which the strictest was a closed-door regime that permitted transfers between wings within the same establishment.

The Arles prison provided one illustration of the conflicts linked to these attempts to implement increasingly strict detention regimes. This prison was closed in 2003 due to flooding. During the renovation work, 4,800 metres of extra barbed wire were placed around the courtyards where prisoners took their strolls, electronic barriers were installed on the roofs of all buildings of less than three floors (the family visit unit, the administration building, workshops). Also, numerous cameras were added, the four accommodation buildings were walled off and a circulation system was introduced that was designed to prevent all contact between prisoners. Upon reopening, a new detention regime was implemented. This was denounced through a prisoner petition and hunger strikes. International Prison Watch reported:

> "The loss of any form of social life in detention (being unable to go to a neighbouring cell to chat, eat meals together...) well beyond the restrictions usually encountered in prisons; pat-down searches every time a prisoner leaves a cell; group movement restricted to two prisoners maximum. Also, family visit conditions allow no social interaction, since they take place in closed boxes, unlike what prevails in penal establishments"[150].

---

149   "Current regulations have reduced constraints on the Correctional Service in the process of prolonging isolation. For example, the Code of Criminal Procedure now provides that an isolation measure becomes exceptional after two years have been spent under this detention regime, as opposed to one year under the previous law" (de Suremain and Bérard 2009).

150   International Prison Watch - French Section, press release, 11 December 2009.

The prefecture responsible for commissioning guards for this prison stated that "the regime is certainly very focused on security, but this results from the choice to have high-security prisons. The Arles prison is initiating what will be applied to prisons that open in the future"[151]. Two of these are under construction.

When the Clairvaux petition was released, Minister of Justice Pascal Clément initially reacted with this remark: "if we took them on their word, how many of them would really come forward?"[152]. This was an effort to depoliticize the action by individualizing this voicing of opinion: "how many of them would really come forward?". It also expresses, more concretely, the resentment of a political fringe that has yet to fully digest the abolition of the death penalty. On 20 October 2006, former Minister of the Interior Charles Pasqua proposed a law on the following grounds:

> "The abolition of the death penalty was pronounced in the autumn of 1981 in the euphoria of a state of grace that, without doubt, was faulty in its excessive optimism or in its one-way sensitivity, that is, in the way it exclusively considered clemency towards criminals. This abolition stemmed from a doctrinarian, unrealistic vision, according to which individuals are not responsible for their actions. The motives that inspired the abolition of the death penalty are incompatible with republican humanism based on the principle of personal responsibility, a foundation of human dignity[153]."

Did this private member's bill advocate a reinstatement of the death penalty? No. It "only" advocated increasing the minimum term to thirty years for some crimes. By means of near-life imprisonment, those who still believed in capital

---

151   *Ibid.*

152   "Pascal Clément detects "manipulation" behind the appeal of the Clairvaux Ten", *AFP*, 25 January 2006.

153   Senate, *Proposition de loi visant à porter la durée de la période de sûreté à trente ans dans les cas de condamnations pour les crimes les plus odieux*, 20 October 2006.

punishment wished to permanently enshrine their revenge against those who advocated the abolition of all never-ending punishment.

By highlighting the gap between the fate they faced and what was expected of the birthplace of human rights, the petitioners shed light on the laconic analysis of Foucault who, on the eve of the abolition of the death penalty, declared that "the real dividing line, among the penal systems, does not pass between those who accept the death penalty and the rest; is passes between those that accept permanent penalties and those who exclude them" (Foucault 2001a, Hartman 2009, Gilbert 2009). For twenty years, European authorities have been explaining that human rights are incompatible with infinite sentences, and have been developing penal and penitentiary standards that take account of the need to prepare prisoners for their return to society, in spite of the destructive effects of lengthy sentences, and to model prison standards as closely as possible on the standards of ordinary law. France is conducting a penal policy that once again legally raises the spectre of true life sentences, and is in fact imposing it on a number of prisoners who, although they could be released under law, either are unable to get released, or see no prospect of being released before they are close to death. By labelling them as dangerous, the CS traps prisoners who participate in struggles.

But France does not want to relinquish its displays of respect for human rights, does not want to acknowledge that its prison laws and parole laws are locked in a struggle against the jurisprudence of European authorities. Through collective expression, prisoners tear away the mask of deception, take ownership of the values their country claims, and trap the government in its own rhetoric, to expose the fact that the universalist human rights label hides a real power struggle between two legal regimes that clash when it comes to fundamental rights.

CHAPTER 7
"After a While, You're Nothing But a Criminal"

I f there is one penal approach that is regularly subject to sharp criticism, it is that which places thousands of petty criminals behind bars every year, sometimes more than once, to serve short sentences. After the prison revolts of 1974, a law on non-custodial sentences was passed[154]. During the parliamentary debates, ultra-conservative MP and former Minister of Justice Jean Foyer explained, as an aside: "If we believe we must to the fullest extent possible prevent short prison sentences from being handed down and executed— and I think we are unanimous on this point..."[155]. In fact, for thirty years, the question of replacing short sentences with other forms of punishment has never stopped being discussed. These discussions contributed to the bipartition of the criminal sanctions system into two distinct branches: so-called "closed custody" (ie. prison), and "open custody", which encompasses all measures said to be "exercised in the community", to use Council of Europe terminology. 142,000 people were handled through open custody in 2007 (Ministère de la Justice 2009). And yet, short sentences have not disappeared. Even worse, despite the fact that after 1980 (96,955 admissions) there was a downward trend in the number of incarcerations (64,730 in 2001), this trend reversed, and a continuous increase was observed between 2001 and 2005 (85,540 in 2005, 90,200 in 2007) (Ministère de la Justice

---

154   Law of 11 July 1975 altering and completing some provisions of penal law.
155   Jean Foyer, National Assembly, 16 May 1975, *Journal Officiel*, p. 2752.

2009). This raised serious doubts about the shift towards so-called "penal bifurcation", which consisted in toughening penalties for some offence categories (sex crimes, violent offences, narcotics offences or recidivism), while at the same time trying to reduce incarceration for those serving short sentences, for those awaiting trial, and for young people (Tubex and Snacken 1996).

Governments that promote increased penal severity have internalized criticism against prison as a form of punishment. But for the occasional exception, they no longer speak of the inherent virtues of imprisonment, beyond that of neutralizing offenders. Penal deterrence theories and prison's neutralization function have thus made it possible to hybridize the new watchword "risk management"[156] with warlike rhetoric against petty offences. So prison is not legitimized solely by means of correctionalism; detention professionals broadly agree that when detention times are short, implementing an effective sentence execution plan is challenging, if not impossible. This renewed legitimization of prison has been integrated into symbolic rhetoric addressed to socially vulnerable groups that possess little means of material and symbolic protection against the nuisance of petty crime. Here David Garland's analysis hits the mark: "A show of punitive force against individuals is used to repress any acknowledgement of the state's inability to control crime to acceptable levels. A willingness to deliver harsh punishments to convicted offenders magically compensates a failure to deliver security to the population at large." (Garland, 1996)

At the same time, this reinvented punitive show neglects rehabilitation in order to resurrect one of the oldest and most regressive strands of modern penal reasoning: deterrence (Pires 1998, Mathiesen 2006). According to the Right, the rules of the game need to be altered when they deem that the negative risk offenders incur is not substantial enough and/or not perceived clearly enough. This is the prevailing logic behind the idea of minimum sentences for repeat offenders, which led to the first penal law of Nicolas Sarkozy's term

---

156   On this point, see chapter 4.

of office. This is the same rationale that makes it possible—despite evidence to the contrary—to assert that legislative laws that boost repression by increasing penalties prevent crime. As the recidivism law was being passed in 2005, did we not hear MP and future UMP Minister Christian Estrosi assert that the imposition of minimum sentences could empty prisons by deterring potential criminals?

As the prisoners themselves testify—and as we will now show—this severity rhetoric is laughable in relation to the logic of a prisoner's existence and the concrete reality of his relationship with prisons and the law. Symbolic deterrence in no way affects the direction people's lives take, except through temporary exclusion and stigmatization. This is precisely why it never stops being reinforced: to show—as right-wing governments keep repeating to those who still have not understood that their behaviour was unacceptable—that this behaviour must stop.

More than any other aspect of the system, the flood of short sentences illustrates how prisons function as a place where popular illegalisms are organized and criminal networks are built. To use Howard Becker's terms, it confirms the rule that "one of the most crucial steps in the process of building a stable pattern of deviant behaviour is likely to be the experience of being caught and publicly labelled as a deviant" (Becker 1966, 31). In this respect, prisoners can teach us more than anyone else about how the institutions really operate, through their practical knowledge and infrapolitical criticism[157].

Prison routine

> "When you're a minor, whether you break into a car or break into a house now and then, they're going to give you a suspended sentence—suspended and then suspended again. Then you've got parole, day parole, stuff like that, you know, community service... But as

---

157   This is one of the supporting principles of "convict criminology". See Ross and Richards (2002), and Ross and Richards (2003).

soon as you're an adult, all your suspended sentences are gone, but they haven't forgotten you. And then you're done for. Usually you go straight to prison."
Interview at a jail with François, 26 years old, eighth incarceration, 2000[158]

The rehabilitative purpose of incarceration instantly loses all meaning insofar as it is part of the control process that precedes and encompasses it (Jobard and Chantraine 2004). Incarceration does not serve to consecrate a mistake, making it into a channel for feelings of guilt, laying the groundwork for some kind of rehabilitation. It rather serves to prolong and intensify contact with police and the penal system. In this context, incarceration bears the mark of ineluctability; it is the culmination of a rationale of routinized monitoring, endless summonses, ritualized confrontation with police authorities, and accumulated convictions.

"I'm supposed to get out on April 21st, but on the morning of April 21st they can come and say 'look, sign your committal order, now go over there and wait for the ruling.' It would be better to tell me right away, but if all goes well, I don't think I'll be placed under a committal order. And yet if I'm supposed to leave on April 22nd, before April 22nd a committal order can be pronounced, then I'd stay here. It could also happen that I get out, then my case comes up in court, and I get a new sentence. As long as I'm not on the other side of the door, I'm not out, that's clear."
Interview at a jail with Gaston, 23 years old, first incarceration, 2001.

During their first incarceration, "new arrivals" experience the prison adage: "You know when you're going in, but you don't know when you're getting out". Since the duration of detention is subject to police, court and prison vagaries, institutionalized uncertainty is a fundamental and essential

158   The interview extracts reproduced here are from Chantraine (2004).

characteristic of jail. It reduces all correctionalist efforts to naught, while conferring on the courts, as Pierre Bourdieu expressed it, "the absolute power (…) to make oneself unpredictable and deny other people any reasonable anticipation, and to place them in total uncertainty by offering no scope to their capacity to predict" (Bourdieu 2000, 228).

In working-class neighbourhoods, young people's mental anchoring on prison is a consequence of penal procedures. Summary trials are being applied more and more widely. Some members of the public prosecutor's office went as far as exalting summary trials because they prevent the accused from preparing a defence: "For the most serious cases, or those of [repeat offenders], there is a summary trial. The defendant must be judged right away. And it has to be simple. A summary trial is an instant blow. The criminal doesn't have time to defend himself." (Bastard, Mouhanna and Ackermann 2005). Incarceration is the logical outcome. The consequence: in 2002, the number of cases pursued though the summary trial procedure (38,300) overtook the number of cases subject to thorough investigation (37,400), and in 2005 the number of prison and jail admissions resulting from the quick procedure (29,500) overtook the number of admissions resulting from "investigations" (28,400).

Contrary to the criminological notion that the study of crime should be confined to the criminal acts of deviant individuals, the sociology of crime inextricably links the analysis of the incrimination process (the creation and changing of penal laws), the analysis of transgression practices, and the analysis of secondary criminalization practices ("concrete" repression, particularly police and judicial practices) (Robert 2005)[159]. And for over thirty years, penal sociology has endeavoured to describe all of the social mechanisms by which populations are selected for penal repression. By analyzing the "funnel-like" functioning of penal procedures—defining offences, sentencing offenders, reporting

---

159   In this sense, the sociology of crime is as much opposed to "conventional criminology" as a set of scholarly prevention principles and practices relating to ontologized and unproblematized objects (crimes, criminals) as it is to "administrative criminology", implicitly or even explicitly imprisoned in the categories of the state apparatus (Carrier and Chantraine 2009).

crimes to authorities, elucidation, selecting legal proceedings and court procedures—it becomes possible to get away from the legalist image of criminal justice as a way of curbing offences defined by the law (Robert 1977; Aubusson de Cavarlay 1985). The study of penal procedures specifically reveals why, through mechanisms that are certainly not fixed (Aubusson de Cavarlay 2005), the police and the law's focus on offences that are visible and subject to urgent trial leads a significant proportion of poor people into prison. According to Bruno Aubusson de Cavarlay's analysis, thirty years ago, a defendant's professional situation strongly influenced the decision to remand him in custody, whereas now this factor appears to apply much less. But recourse to summary trials has a retroactive effect on police work. The impact of the defendant's social standing is smallest at the moment of judgement, but it is decisive before this. With the exception of a small percentage of drunk driving cases, which involve people from all walks of life, summary trials serve to deal with visible crime, such as violent thefts witnessed by police. These offences are a fact of life for a population without jobs, often living in the streets, and towards whom police work is directed. These people are speedily convicted for street offences, making frequent return tips between the inside and outside.

"It's a routine. When you come here for the first time, it shocks you, it even subdues you. But after, they drag you down more and more. Even all the guards, when they see me, I know them, it's a routine. What they do is stupid. It's a joke."
Interview at a jail with Justin, 23 years old, eleventh incarceration, 2000.

Some judges think that when they hear a summary trial, the personality of the defendant can be reduced to his criminal record, and the context in which the alleged acts took place cannot really be considered. This is another way of saying that the fact of having committed a repeat offence is the only criterion that comes into play when determining a sentence. Judges who support this conviction method say it is a practical necessity that deals with the petty crimes blocking up the courts, to which the law is called upon to bring a "penal response". But it is justified more ideologically by the desire for a gradation of penalties that does not reverse in the case of repeat offences, since its deterrent effect would be ruined. In other words, although a suspended sentence can make an impression on a first-time defendant and discourage him from repeating the offence, it is completely unrealistic to expect to turn a multiple offender who has already been to prison away from crime in this way; the only solution is to show him that the penalties will become tougher every time. From the "Safety and Freedom" law (*"Sécurité and liberté"* 1981) to the most recent recidivism laws, this reasoning has contributed to a growing crackdown on repeat offenders. "When the outside security of the French people is based on deterrence, why would internal security pooh-pooh this? The feeling of being unsafe is nevertheless fuelled by criminals who are engaged in a kind of private war with their compatriots." This defence of the deterrent virtues of heavier sentences was made on 11 June 1980 by then-Minister of Justice Alain Peyrefitte. He was defending his "Safety and Freedom" law before Parliament, part of which was dedicated to toughening sentences for repeat offenders. He explained that we must put an end to *"lottery justice"*, which takes the *"culprit's psychology"* into consideration, and return to a fundamental principle: *"that the culprit pays back society, whatever the price"*. Recent statistics on previous convicts returning to prison for "petty offences" debunks the hypothesis that prison or jail has become—by what miracle?—rehabilitative of the criminals the courts keep sending there. For example, among the people released from prison and jail in 1996/1997 after serving time for non-violent thefts, 75% of them had been convicted again within five years, and 65% had received stiff prison or jail sentences (Kensey and Tournier 2004).

"You adapt to the place. Personally, right now, where I stand, you can put me in jail, but I don't know what jail is anymore; I don't know what jail is!"
Interview at a jail with Daniel, 27 years old, fifth incarceration, 2001.

The constant coming and going in and out of jail enables the circulation of information about notable events in jail and in the neighbourhood, a solidarity between individuals of the same neighbourhood as well as protection against violence in detention. The network of neighbourhood connections is reassuring; it attenuates the fear of the individual in detention. "Preparation" for incarceration and attempts to manage its adverse affects are routinized, as are the ways of killing time in detention. As one prisoner who had just returned to jail said: "*I'm taking a metalwork course again, the same as usual*" (François, 26 years old, eighth incarceration, interview conducted at a jail in 2000). Prisoners develop a personal acquaintance with the guards, and this can provide various minor privileges, such as access to work or an extra shower. Returning to jail means being reunited with neighbourhood friends. Jail and the neighbourhood are symbolically connected[160]. As one person we interviewed explained during a recent study of a poor neighbourhood:

"I've spent a lot of time in prison. In prison, you're forced to live with people. You can become best buddies with someone, spend your days with him, but you can't have faith in it. You have to watch your back. If he can take something from you, he will. You can never show weakness. Well, the neighbourhood is the same. You can't trust anyone. Especially when it comes to business. That's why trafficking is organized more and more within families. At least with your brother and your cousin you can be a bit surer. As I often say in the neighbourhood, prison has its own culture. Especially among young people. It's like in prison, it's organized into groups"[161].

160   See also Wacquant (2001).
161   Ali, 46 years old, former drug trafficker, quoted in (Lapeyronnie 2008, 487).

The same study concluded that "the law, which weighs on many individuals and families, obviously affects life in the whole ghetto. Lots of young people have been arrested and arraigned for criminal acts. Practically everyone has a brother or friend, at least one acquaintance from their immediate circle, who has had dealings with the justice system and prison" (Lapeyronnie 2008, 288).

Confinement trajectories

A recent study (Chantraine 2008)[162] examining the social trajectories of incarcerated minors showed that for practically all incarcerated youths, prison only acquires meaning as part of a "confinement trajectory". This notion does not solely apply to the trajectories of people in detention (the shock of the arrival, adaptation, preparation for release), nor solely to the institutional confinement (CER, CEF) that might precede or follow detention. The "confinement trajectory" more fundamentally characterizes how the social paths of young people are recounted as if they were inescapable *destinies*. Territorial confinement, biographical confinement, institutional confinement: the narratives are structured around the inability to swap one's life for another[163]. For young people whose institutional paths end in prison, the different types of custody under the Youth Judicial Protection Service are not seen as a way of avoiding penalties, they are regarded as yet another social constraint, one of the biographical junction stations leading—slowly but surely—to incarceration.

Other studies supplement this observation, enabling a better understanding of the biographical ineluctability that looms over every prison stay. At the end of a path scattered with placements in social institutions and contacts with the penal system, incarceration, far from engendering

---

162   Here we present a few results from the study, as conducted by Chantraine (2009b): http://www.cesdip.fr/spip.php?article417.

163   Often "delinquent professionalization"—advancing from street delinquency to a more profitable, better organized delinquency—is narratively presented as taking control of one's life.

a desire to rehabilitate, constructs criminal networks by making the experience part of collective everyday life (Le Caisne 2008). We agree with Yahyâ Hachem Samii's analysis, here applied to Belgium: "[Imprisoned minors] always expressed disillusionment and outrage, experiencing their situation as the logical conclusion of their history and as a supplementary injustice. Having become 'delinquents', they are summing up their story as written by the protection services, that is to say, as a long series of events building up to the offence. That being the case, why listen to words intended to make you feel guilty or respond to punishment if the trajectory is unavoidable in any case?" (Hachem Samii 2005). Biographical interviews show a "destiny effect", which can assume a personal, collective, and/or familial form.

> "Personally, I steal simply because... I have no money... I have no work... I don't have anything! So to be honest, that's all I have... I steal because I don't have money. Simple as that! And I know that if I get out in September, I'll do it again, I'm telling you! I know that if I get out in September, I won't do an apprenticeship... I won't have a penny! The next day I'll steal... and steal again... but that's what I always did... I've already been out several times and the next day, that's what I did...".
>
> Interview with Hafiz, 17 years old,
> 3rd incarceration, minor's wing of a jail, 2007.

Incarcerated minors mainly stress their multiple disadvantages: poverty, lack of schooling, rootlessness, multiple convictions linked to the delinquency of poverty and the need to survive. At the heart of their stories, delinquency and its specific pleasures (adrenaline, money, living it up) can be presented as "choices", but this is the story of a limited choice. Occasionally mentioned as an alternative is the (rejected) prospect of an honest but impoverished life.

"I went to meetings right away to find work... Never heard from them again! You just wait around. The usual routine... it's like before... and just like before, it doesn't do any good... I have some community service work, but in a month I'll have nothing to do... I have to find things to do, or else... [...] I'll sell a bit of dope. It's all about getting a few pennies in my pockets... [...] Even if I don't want to do anything stupid, I know myself... I'll start working, then something happens and I'll say fuck it, and drop everything... I don't give a shit.... I can't say prison has made me stop doing stupid things. For now I've stopped, but I can't say that I've really stopped.... because if something happens and I have to do whatever's necessary... In fact, it wasn't prison that made me stop... I wasn't happy about being there, I was disgusted... but anyway, I say that now, but tomorrow I still might go and steal something... that's why you don't know, why you can't know... that's what'll happen on the street".

Interview with Adrien, 16 years old,
first incarceration, minor's wing in a jail, 2007.

In this context, the ineluctability narrative can be perceived in two ways. Either it is explicit: the young person clearly states that he knew he was going to end up in prison, that there was no avoiding it; or it is implicit, which perhaps further reinforces its sociological significance. Ineluctability is not presented as such, but it is, in fact, integrated into the *order of things*. The actors' tactics, strategies and resistances, as well as his "choices", become part of a more comprehensive narrative that negates them. For example: a first detention takes place after several convictions and possibly some stays in either young offenders' homes or a restrictive institution such as a CEF[164], and this naturally integrates into the narrative. It is striking to observe the hatred young people feel for the homes they first encountered, which they say were unsafe and encouraged crime, and therefore constituted biographical transfer stations on

---

164   *Centre d'éducation fermé* (closed education centre).

the way to prison (Carra 1996). In other situations, young people perceive incarceration as inevitable (for example as the consequence of a drift towards crime), but it enables them to "put the brakes on"—a young person here making his own use of words often uttered by teachers and judges. Incarceration might make young people consider a change of direction, but as we will detail later, it does not necessarily provide them with the social levers necessary for true social integration.

Léonore Le Caisne's study of prison sociability provided a good description of how young people reconstruct their individual, legal and prison paths in the context of a collective experience. The collective nature of prison experience can manifest itself in the importance of the "reunions" that take place upon a prisoner's arrival and throughout his stay. By attributing a collective dimension to what they are experiencing, minors are able to attenuate the seriousness of their prison experience: "they try to place their presence in prison in a less dramatic perspective and draw attention away from their individual experience and history, integrating these into the culture and way of life of a certain class of young people" (Le Caisne 2008, 53). Thus, "boys build communities of symbolic affinity that enable them to explain their behaviour without having to question themselves." (Le Caisne 2008, 88)[165].

As this study shows, the ties that bind prisoners are so strong that the outside culture they bring into detention is little affected. As a result, the institution still only has a limited effect on young people. The reunions allow them to assemble a peer group that provides prestige and social strength within prison and also establishes a bridge between the inside and the outside. Links between prisoners provide protection against the totalizing nature of prison, since it limits the depersonalizing and stigmatizing effects it can engender.

The collective nature of their experiences also enables them to anticipate future incarcerations. Young people can quite precisely compare the forms of organization that

---

165   See also Hachem Samii, (2005, 167).

exist in the separate wings for minors and adults, in terms of prisoner-guard relations, activities offered, rights, etc. Collectivizing the experience allows them to have anticipatory knowledge of adult detention. Others believe that, on the contrary, serving time in prison as a minor will probably help them avoid returning as an adult: "it's better to do stupid things now!". Never having imagined a life without prison, it is simply a matter of preparing to avoid the worst.

Finally, sharing experience enables "those who have come to prison for nothing" and those who have come for "lots of money" to be brought together, evincing, among other things, a process of delinquent professionalization, which is all about leaving behind the delinquency of poverty and regaining the initiative of one's own trajectory by directing one's efforts towards more lucrative activities with more certain outcomes. This collective destiny finds paridigmatic expression when some young people say that prison is necessary "to become a man". Prison then constitutes a genuine *rite of passage*, necessary for building and proving one's virility.

Other actors appear in their narratives: an uncle, brother or father who spent time in prison, sometimes several times, sometime serving long sentences. This family dimension then reinforces the collective dimension of the destiny effect. It also gives young people the idea that probably someday they will stop coming back to prison. The (distant) prospect of breaking free of the prison trajectory paradoxically reinforces both the trajectory's usual course and the idea that one cannot act upon it; it must go where it goes, right to the end. The family destiny reveals other typical prison trajectories that individuals can cite, such as the brother "who got out" and now "has a wife, a job and a car".

In the context of our study of the biographical trajectories of incarcerated minors, a second series of interviews provided an opportunity to ask young prisoners about the direction their lives took after they left prison. These interviews show that, whether prison is recounted as an ineluctable experience or as a biographical rupture, it is in no case a step that brings a social-judicial trajectory to a close. The detention period is no longer a way of settling accounts with the law, it is a time when the young person's social and penal trajectory is reorganized. Detention reduces penal uncertainty. In fact, although this often exists before incarceration, it is nevertheless reinforced under the weight of an ever more prominent prison threat; young people know that they risk landing back in prison, either for the same crime or for another, but they do not know when or for how long.

Incarceration also produces biographical and existential dead-ends. There are many narratives that stress the "desire to integrate", the wish not to return to prison, etc. But these statements seem to be either just the done thing (it is the story one "must" tell), or they are disconnected from the actors' real capacity for initiative. It is this disparity between hopes and objective life conditions that explains why the narratives are often structured by total ambivalence: on the one hand a desire to integrate, on the other hand the fear of returning to prison and the feeling that this return to prison is possible, even probable. In light of these uncertainties and dead ends, prison may be perceived as pointless (it in no way changes the conditions that determined the direction the young person took), as productive of dead ends (recidivism is considered inevitable), as leading to crime (it enables delinquent professionalization; it hardens people), and as stigmatizing (therefore making individuals vulnerable).

A nonexpert criminology

Prisoners, whether adults or minors, are the first to point out the meaninglessness of penalties handed down urgently and served in jails that are inevitably crowded and idle. Although they cannot express this criticism during the judicial ritual itself, behind the scenes many of them denounce the gap between judicial rhetoric and the application of the law, between the legal and the sociological, between justice and prison "as they should be" and "as they are", backing up their criticism with individual and collective experience.

One person denounces the impoverishment that followed his incarceration, for himself and for his family, demonstrating the counterproductive nature of prison as an institution that causes destitution. Another person denounces the obstacle that a criminal record presents, its very existence reducing the principle of rehabilitation to ideological rhetoric that masks a vast stigmatizing machine. Yet another describes the illogic of compelling jailed defendants to endure the most difficult living conditions even though they are presumed innocent; yet another describes losing his job and his friends, a loss that plunged him into a criminal environment were people were eager to share effective criminal techniques, etc.

More generally, faced with the seeming ineluctability of their path, their criticism assumes two configurations, sometimes both found in the same person. In the first configuration, the "system" seems like an intangible apparatus with which one has long maintained a close social and biographical association, and it is a matter of "making do" (trying not to get caught, making this or that statement before the judge, doing what you can to get tobacco while in detention, etc.). Social and judicial restrictions and the penal system are components of the social world of these individuals; no other world is imagined. One may observe tactical resistance and peripheral criticism (this or that decision by the judge is described as absurd, this or that arbitrary act in detention is criticized, this or that sentence is described as excessive or as coming "out of left field"), but the encompassing social world is rarely questioned more broadly. In the second configuration, on the contrary, one observes a gradual politicization of the analysis of the criminal experience. Then within these stories appear: "the state", "France", which deserves to be "fucked". Some repressive policies are harshly criticized, as is the lack of opportunities offered to "city youth".

> "After a while, you're nothing but a criminal."
> Interview at a jail with François, 26 years old, eighth incarceration, 2000.

Detention conditions are obviously denounced vigorously by the prisoners themselves: the third-rate healthcare system, the lack of labour law, sexual frustrations, crowded cells, ineffective "preparation for release", isolation wings. Even the poor quality of visiting rooms is experienced as a flagrant injustice that the system could do without. Despite the stamp of illegitimacy that marks this criticism and keeps it from being publicized, it is connected to a broader critique of how the criminal justice system operates. This ordinary criminology takes judicial rhetoric on its word when it asserts that everyone is equal before the law; reality is measured against this principle of social justice. The gap between principle and reality haunts everyday life in detention, and for the prisoners, it drives the politicization of illegalisms, of a radical fatalism, of hopelessness and rebellion. During long discussions in cells, systematic and thorough comparison between cases and between experiences with the penal process as a whole (relations with police officers, entering the prison register, the investigation, judgement and sentence execution) resemble—in the ability to establish equivalencies and make generalizations—the mental processes of criminologists, sometimes yielding very similar results[166].

At the heart of this infrapolitical criminology, essentially structured around the idea of differential judicial treatment, three more specific criticisms emerge. Justice is first of all denounced as class justice:

> You know, this sentence is a high price to pay. Two years is a lot. If it had been someone else, you know how much he would have gotten. He would have been given six months, eight at the most. Because of my previous convictions they gave me two years. When the prosecutor stood up, she said (in a cartoonish voice) "Yeah, I beg the court, against Mr. A...".

---

166   Links between expert criminology and nonexpert criminology, as well as the latter's relation to the politicization of illegalisms in detention, are more fully detailed in Chantraine (2004), chapter 4, "Professionnalisation : réaffiliation, carrière, révolte".

Because it's a theatre. I'm telling you straight, as far as I'm concerned it's theatre... and then the lawyer arrives... But I need the law, because if there were no laws there would be anarchy, everyone would shoot everyone else. We need the law, but it's a law people scoff at, because it's a two-tier law. You have one law for the rich, and one law for the poor.

Interview at a jail with Adil, 31 years old, eighth incarceration, 2001.

The justice system is also perceived as racist:

As long as you don't see the justice system up close, you can't understand. They judge you more on your past than on the case itself. They tell you "this guy has the habit". They crush us. And me in particular, as an immigrant child... We get bled. In my mind, that's how I think, you know. I've seen the justice system up close, I've been back to prison several times, I understand that it's not right. The judge can be very good... saying "I'm not racist...", but, you know, unconsciously, when they judge you, they tell themselves that this guy's not European. If you look at the statistics, you can take ten immigrants, from whatever background, whether they're black or... And then you take ten French people. You try them for the same crimes, similar crimes, you hand down a judgement, then you'll see the conclusions, convincing ones... I'm telling you, that's how it is. I'm not saying it's racism, but I'm saying they have a tendency to apply the law more harshly to people like me.

Interview with Miloud, 29 years old, at an outside placement training centre, around ten incarcerations, 2001.

Finally, a number of those interviewed compared justice to a lottery. There are a few factors that prevent this lottery from being completely given over to chance, but these constitute supplementary sources of inequality. Two examples are trial location (when drugs violations were involved, many prisoners explained that they would have received lighter or heavier sentences depending on the region in which they were tried) and the discretionary power of the judge, who distributes sentences according to his own goodwill (a goodwill influenced by his political views and his opinion of what is needed to curb offences[167]).

> I ended up with a really repressive judge. Because it's usually the prosecutor who asks for the most, an exemplary sentence, and the judge usually asks for less. I'd heard of community service, and I told myself "ok, that's fine, I'll be outside". The decision: "six months in jail!" So I don't know about justice. Because some of the people involved in my case—there were seven of us—some of them were given a year, I got six months, and the third, he was tried as the street dealer, even though he's a repeat offender, and he's already been given two years for the same crimes. And it's my first offence. That's why there's something illogical about justice.
>
> Interview at a jail with Gaston, 23 years old, first detention, 2000.

Here we see an extreme concretization of a conception of domination identified by D. Martuccelli, who, with the help of J. C. Scott, points out that the dominated are less fettered at the level of thought and speech than at the level of action and political struggle (Scott 1990; Martucelli 2004)[168]. The individual detention experience is marked

---

167   In this sense, this type of criticism agrees not only with that of some sociologists or criminologists, but also with that of some political leaders who want to limit the political risk presented by the relative independence of judges.

168   Martucelli stresses that analysis of the cognitive conceptions of the dominated should not be limited to a set of critical postures, and more generally stresses that the imaginary and discursive world of the dominated always eludes the grip of a homogeneous cultural inculcation: "domination can impose the practical consent of the dominated, not voluntary consent". It is thus that one must reconstruct the stories of the "fearsome life" (a penchant for risk, showing off, nightlife, casual sex, adventure, quality drugs and wealth) that interweave, in one single biographical narrative, with those of hardship, and of the "irreversible path". See Chantraine (2004, 99-106).

by an abysmal gulf between the prisoners' critical abilities and the pressure to submit to prison rules. One ex-prisoner who had been depressed since his release and found it difficult to enumerate his psychological and social problems summed it up thus: "in prison, you have the ability to think, but if you have nothing to do, thinking screws up something inside you".

In this context, committing crime can also be conceived as one way of rejecting an unjust and absurd order that grants power, happiness and wealth to some, and a life of poverty and toil to others.

I don't understand how the average person can accept living the life that's been forced on him. I don't understand that. My father worked all his life, to be able to retire. I won't tell you the problems he had because he hadn't kept his payslips... He never got involved with the law, he had always been straight... Anyway, people see clearly, there are demonstrations because people really understand that politicians don't give a damn about them. When you see the layoffs, the factories closing, what is that? Why? It's a question of interest, a question of money, that's all. They have to stop taking people for idiots. But now I think people, since they started working, they've been fooled by the system, they've had so much forced on them, on their way of seeing how that system should work. They settle for it, they get to the point that they settle for that. Well, all the better for them, but personally, I can't live like that, I could never live like that. I'm a free man. I'm in prison, but I'm free. I could never...

[...] All I wish for, one of these days, is to have, I don't know, a platform, a debate, to explain to them that they have to stop their foolishness, their system, what they do... There would be other solutions, simpler ones, to make it so a man doesn't leave prison in this condition. Confining people in prison like that isn't a solution, it just makes things worse and worse. But I think it's done on purpose, in fact it's part of the legal system.

Interview at a jail with Julien, 36 years old, fifth incarceration, 2001.

So prison is conceived as the institution that "makes the system work", that reproduces absurd inequalities while mentally and physically crushing those who attempt to upset the existing order. The idea that "prison is made to destroy" imposes itself.

A study from the early 1980s (Montandon and Crettaz 1981) had already highlighted some prisoner conceptions: the police force was considered a relatively violent body, lawyers were useless scroungers, psychiatric experts were full of jargon, distorting reality. More generally, it revealed a system of argumentation used by prisoners to denounce inequality before the law: doubting the impartiality of judges and deconstructing the subtle mechanisms that influence legislators. The authors then pointed out a problem that still exists: although it was surprising that the prisoners should praise the criminal justice system overall, it is hard to believe that the deep injustice prisoners feel will never lead to a profound disrespect that could turn out to be largely counterproductive in terms of the penal system's official purpose. Although prison is presented as justice itself and as a reminder of the law, it in fact engenders extreme scepticism and a deep feeling of injustice among inmates. In their eyes, the system automatically disqualifies itself through its everyday practices. There is too great a contrast between the legitimate, legal depiction of time in prison—as punishment for a deviant act enabling a return to a life without crime—and the social and institutional experiences of people who move from prison into state social organisations that assist and manage the poorest people. This is what we examine in our final chapter.

CHAPTER 8
Out of One Prison, Into Another

I n the 1970s, there were protest movements critical of the incarceration of casual workers, of chicken and moped thieves, and of immigrants, who were treated harshly by a justice system denounced as classist and racist: "a young man accused of having stolen a 100-franc note in a cafe is sentenced to four months in jail, the judge reproaching him above all for having quit his job in Verdun"; "an unemployed person or immigrant will have no chance of convincing the court that he found a valuable object"; "Anyone belonging to what the prosecutor calls the 'unsettled population' is considered a potential criminal"[169]. A 2002 study by the National Institute of Statistics and Economic Studies (the INSEE[170]) directly echoed these denouncements and the analyses of J-G. Petit, who described convicts of the second half of the 19th century as defeated people, social rejects produced by new demographic and industrial changes, poor country people or uprooted proletarians with non-existent or insubstantial family connections (Petit 1998). According to the INSEE study, among prisoners, aside from those who had left school early, working-class men were greatly overrepresented. They had generally received only a limited education. Over a quarter of them had left school before the age of thirteen, three-quarters before the age of eighteen. Among men incarcerated less than thirty years, half had stopped studying

---

169 *Tout !*, no. 1, 23 September 1970.
170 L'Institut national de la statistique et des études économiques.

before the age of eighteen, three years earlier than the national average. At any given age, the risk of being incarcerated greatly decreases the longer the individual spent in school. A look at parents' professions confirms the overrepresentation of the working class: 47% of prisoners' fathers are labourers, 16% are artisans or merchants. More than half of mothers are not employed, and those who are employed often work as cleaners or service staff. Finally, the relationship to work is key as well; one in seven prisoners has never had an job, and half of them are or were labourers, compared with one third in the general population. The study shows that many prisoners come from large families; more than half of them have four siblings or more, as compared with under one third for the male population as a whole. One in twenty comes from a family of more than ten children (INSEE 2002).

In the context of a study on the work of an association supporting poor released prisoners (Bérard 2011), two volunteers, after detailing the case of someone they had helped, used the same expression: "it's terrible".

> One prisoner [a former teacher] said to me "I'm all alone and I'm comfortable, but every day I'm afraid, just over going to the visiting room, I'm constantly turning back, I try to choose the times". He had given me the schedule because there were times when he couldn't go into the hallway without fear of being beaten up. This is a very heavy, burdensome reality. Even if these people are only jailed for fifteen days, it can change a guy in a terrible way: the lack of freedom, living with others, the people around them, the pace of life, relationships or the lack thereof. [...] All of this means that really, as soon as they get out it's terrible, they're lost. They want to get out but they dread it: what time will they get out? Who will be waiting for them? How will people look at them? Will they find work? Has their wife left them? Most of the time the answer is yes. Will they find a place to live? [...] It's terrible.
>
> Interview with the local head of a prison visitor's association, 2010.

"There was one person who knew about us and came to the association. We chatted and then started a support program. He brought me a suitcase with all of his papers in disorder. He had his life in that suitcase. I don't know how he managed. It was a guy who'd been on the streets several times, and also in prison, and he was waiting for his papers. He was an immigrant. So he had this suitcase full of papers. He was also housed [in a shelter]. He was sick of not seeing anyone when he got out, so he came to the association when he was released from prison. I sent him to an integration workshop. He had to prove one year of work to sort out his status and he was a long way from getting a job. He's around 35. Now he repairs household appliances. He's sorted out his papers and his healthcare benefits. Everything had to be redone. He'd been out for three weeks, and he had no idea what he was going to do. There was no direction or goal. It's terrible."

Interview with a support worker, 2011.

These interviews illustrate consistent features of release from prison: stigmatization, broken or weakened family ties, distress over the lack of work and housing. They also show how a release from prison gets caught up in the most recent developments. In the first case, a person who had a stable social situation was convicted of a sexual offence, suffered the particular stigmatization attached to acts of this nature, and lived in a new prison that terrified him. In the second case, a street person had to simultaneously face poverty and the question of his papers and his legal status as an immigrant in France. The assistance he received did not orient him towards an industrial job, but rather towards current forms of social economy, through subsidized employment as part of a reintegration program.

The sociological consistency seen in the recruitment of the majority of prisoners should not, however, obscure a change that concerns not just poor people entangled in the criminal justice system, but poor people in general. The disciplinary model that gave rise to prisons was that of the factory (Melossi and Pavarini 1981), and the image of the prisoner requiring rehabilitation was that of the "bad poor person" (Petit 1998), who rejects the constraints of industrial work. The crisis of this model itself, and the beginning of the era of social precariousness (Castel 2003), challenges this conception of release from prison, particularly because what awaits released prisoners who wish to obey the law is not so much the rigours of work as the ins and outs of waiting for work, temporary employment and precarious housing solutions. One hears these problems echoed in discussions of penitentiary law relating to sentence adjustments, specifically regarding the traditional approval criteria: employment and housing. In the Senate, Nicole Borvo Cohen-Seat stressed "the importance of the question of the lack of stable accommodation. [...]: 17% of new prisoners have no social protection, 5% have no shelter and 10% live in unstable lodgings"[171]. At the same time, UMP deputy Etienne Pinte explained to the National Assembly that during an assignment related to emergency shelter and council housing, he could not help noticing that "a certain number of former prisoners found themselves in the streets because nothing had been planned to prevent this"[172]. His observation was corroborated by Serge Paugam, who showed that one third of people housed in social rehabilitation centres[173] had served time in prison (Paugam 2005).

These social issues enter the penal sphere through the difficulties of meeting the criteria for early release: access to housing and employment. The instability of employment opportunities offered to people in situations of hardship is illustrated by the solutions sought by the rehabilitation and probation services:

> The difficulty we've had is to try and push through a sentence adjustment rehabilitation plan that isn't exclusively based on employment, or if it is based on this, then the employment isn't necessarily stable.

---

171   Nicole Borvo Cohen-Seat, Senate, 6 March 2009.
172   Etienne Pinte, National Assembly, 15 September 2009.
173   *Centres d'hébergement et de réinsertion sociale* (CHRS).

We're dealing more with temporary contracts, knowing that in practice, judges want the contract to last as long as the sentence adjustment. But ever so slowly, this is starting to slide too, if the plan offers other guarantees. I'm thinking of a prisoner on a semi-release, who has temporary posts that follow one another, not necessarily systematically one day after the next. Since he's semi-released, housing is not an issue.

Interview with the director of a rehabilitation and probation service, 2010.

The second basic approval criterion is also difficult to satisfy. As Daniel Terrolle and Patrick Gaboriau have explained, using data from the Abbé Pierre Foundation, "the inadequacy of available housing is rooted in the 'deficit accumulated during the 1976-1998 period (600 000 homes), and this was not absorbed by the resumption of construction in the late 1990s'" (Gaboriau and Terrolle 2007). The growing incompatibility between prisoners' situations and sentence adjustment approval criteria was exposed by a study undertaken by the National Consultative Commission on Human Rights (CNCDH[174]), which was itself based on analyses made by the probation service. They cite the views of practitioners like Jean-Pierre Bailly, director of the Rehabilitation and Parole Services in Yvelines, who said that these approval conditions "are still formatted according to 'bourgeois rehabilitation' standards, which means stable work and housing". He believes that a "significant portion of the prison population is no doubt able to stop committing crimes, but is incapable of entering this rehabilitation scheme"[175]. In a similar vein, Philippe Pottier believes that the purpose of punishment, and the Correctional Service's task, "is not to normalize people according to rehabilitation criteria that some people could never satisfy without reoffending". He also points out the absurdity "of requiring prisoners to find work before obtaining a parole, when if they

174 *Commission nationale consultative des droits de l'homme* (CNCDH).
175 Jean-Pierre Bailly, director of the SPIP in Yvelines, hearing by the CNCDH, 4 April 2006.

worked before, incarceration would have caused them to lose their job"[176]. He believes the justice system sends a "totally contradictory message to convicts" (CNCDH 2007b).

This data raises specific questions relating to sentence adjustments. Can a squat be considered a home in the context of an adjustment request? Is a temporary job that covers only part of the period of the follow-up plan valid for such a request? The law attempted to respond to this point by partially changing the approval criteria relating to work: "Article 82 re-wrote the parole approval criteria that were provided for the conditional releases that were provided for under article 729 of the Code of Criminal Procedure, which are now possible for any convict participating in a serious integration or rehabilitation plan"[177]. As Michèle Alliot-Marie explains, "in a period of crisis, when there is an appreciable rise in the unemployment rate, it is difficult to subject sentence adjustment approvals to a *sine qua non* condition. So it seems to me that it should be conditioned upon a 'serious integration plan' instead"[178]. In other words, the penal system's internal deliberations bring a broader sociological issue into relief, in the sense that releasing the poorest prisoners raises questions that are as much linked to incarceration itself as to the forms of restriction and discipline that define their lives on the outside and must be confronted.

On the basis of these observations, we are inclined to treat the precarious lives we describe as *forms of confinement*. In other words, we will take seriously the refusal of some prisoners to accept releases that have been arranged in collective accommodation, a refusal that is not so much indicative of pathologies, shortcomings or the denial of reality, but points to the reality of *what is not tolerated* in

---

176   Philippe Pottier, director of the SPIP in Essonne at the time of the hearing, assistant to the Deputy Director of persons placed under the control of the justice system in the Correctional Service Administration, President of the French Society of Criminology, hearing by the National Consultative Commission on Human Rights, 27 April 2006.

177   Circular by the Department of Criminal Affairs and Pardons, 1 December 2009, relating to the first presentation of penitentiary law no. 20091436 of 24 November 2009, altering the Penal Code and the Code of Criminal Procedure.

178   Michèle Alliot-Marie, National Assembly, 15 September 2009.

these ways of handling prisoners, and is expressed in the form of a prison analogy. We are addressing a point that lies beyond the scope of the Correctional Service, the justice system and prison policy debates. This is how professionals and volunteers responsible for preparing the poorest prisoners express their pessimism:

> "When you hear a tutor or someone from the SPIP[179] say: 'we put this guy back on his feet, but when he's released he'll have nothing, he'll go back downhill... you see that it's not prison that kills, it's what comes before and after prison'".

> I've seen quite a few leave prison. I've seen people scared to death of leaving prison, I'm not kidding. I'm thinking of one guy, someone who was in for minor offences: blood-alcohol level, driving without a license. He was scared to death. He didn't know where to go, he didn't have any work. He said 'I'll go downhill again', he was scared to death".
> Interview with a volunteer prison visitor, 2010

Released prisoner support: the tale of a typical trajectory

At the end of *Les Naufragés*, a book about the homeless that generated substantial media interest, Patrick Declerck told a story that is typical of the support worker/client relationship when it involves the "serious social outcasts" that "tramps" are. He described three distinct phases. The first is "the development of the therapeutic plan". This is characterized by a kind of "honeymoon period [...] when the client and support worker seem to reach an agreement on therapeutic objectives and means" (Declerck 2001, 350). Their unity of purpose allows them to develop operational plans. On the one hand, "the potential success of the project makes the client feel better", on the other, the support worker is

---

179   *Service pénitentiaire d'insertion et de probation* (Rehabilitation and Parole Services).

"comforted in his belief in the effectiveness of his power and the legitimacy of the action he is taking". It is during a second phase—that of "implementation"—that "things get spoiled". On the one hand, "since the client is asking for papers, a drug withdrawal treatment, accommodation and a training course, the support worker mobilizes existing resources to provide him with these papers, that treatment, this accommodation and that course". On the other hand, this formalization of needs is based on a "profound misunderstanding", which leads to a "growing dissonance between the client's expressed desires and his real options" (Declerck 2001, 352), which is aggravated by the pathological dimension of desocialization. This leads to the appearance of "pragmatic dissonances": "various tasks left undone, appointments missed, accidents, somatization, drug addiction relapses, suicide attempts". Then the final phase gets underway: the "abandonment" of the relationship. Support workers "often feel betrayed by patients, who turn out not to be what they said they were" (Declerck 2001, 353). And for the client, "the relationship with the support worker is soon experienced as something stifling". In different ways, particularly depending on the institutional context in which the relationship takes place, this abandonment leads to the "breaking of the link" (Declerck 2001, 353).

Patrick Declerck's catastrophic description, which supported the idea that this type of relationship was doomed to failure, was severely criticized by other sociologists (Gardella 2001; Soutrenon 2005), and the relationship between a volunteer support worker and a prisoner is certainly different from a therapeutic relationship, though the similarity of the issues encountered makes it possible to compare this model to the experience of a support worker.

Here it is worth quoting at length a support worker's thoughts about a first visit, related during an extensive interview:

How do you think it went?
To me it was amazing, really satisfying. It's great. I met this young guy, a nice guy. I think we should do everything

possible to get him out of there. He gets out next week. What he lacks is housing and work. Well, he did send me down the wrong track by telling me he was going to be hired [through an rehabilitation organization], and I phoned [this organization] but unfortunately they had nothing lined up for him. We definitely need to find him a place to live [...]. We'll find him something, I think, but probably no earlier than May or June.

In fact, the person you met was a pleasant surprise?
Yes absolutely, completely.

He hadn't prepared anything with the Rehabilitation and parole services?
No, no.

Did he explain why?
Yes, he lived in a squat with three friends for three years, and they spent their time getting plastered— there's no other way of putting it. He got sick because of that, epilepsy caused by alcohol. He's not epileptic, so he understood that he was destroying himself, that he could do better.

Are there any employment prospects?
[Yes, through] an association that helps rehabilitate young people. Cleaning forests, riverbanks. It's something he'd really enjoy. It's great, you're outside, there's contact with nature. I think it's not a bad way to begin rehabilitation.

Would this start in the next few weeks or months?
Around May or June, yes.

And what about housing?
For that, a few of us are trying to make inquiries at the CCAS[180], either in [city], or [at the hostel] in [city]. [...]

---

180   *Centre communal d'action sociale* (Communal Social Welfare Centre).

Will you see him again when he's released?
I'm going to pick him up the day he's released. He was delightful.

Interview with a support worker, a part-time doctor nearing retirement, his first experience with the prison system[181].

During this first meeting, the support worker reflected on this man's isolation, and on the complete lack of preparation for his release.

He hadn't planned anything for his release. The little family he has live in Champagne. He has no family, no partner, his squat friends aren't motivated to do much beyond getting drunk together. They're not very motivated. When he left prison, no one was waiting for him. That's the hardest thing. I really wanted to be there so when the prison door opened, like you see in films, instead of facing an empty street, there's someone who's come to get you.

Release marks the beginning of difficulties, through two challenges. The first consists in the support worker convincing the person to contact the emergency accommodation centre where he believes a place has been reserved.

He had nothing. He was given a small tent when he left, you know, a small tent to go and sleep in. I didn't know they did that. I was surprised. [...] The prisoner said to me: "They [the welfare centre] put in a word for me, they said to go [to the emergency accommodation centre]. I phoned them and they said you're expected, we'll see you, we'll give you a room". I thought "that's perfect, that's great". That's what he told me the first time I saw him. When he left prison, I told him we'd go [to the emergency accommodation centre]. He said: "No, I don't want to leave prison only to go to

---

181   Unless otherwise indicated, the quotations in this section are from this interview.

another one". Oh really? "Because [at the emergency accommodation centre], there are rules, schedules, you can't do this, you can't do that".

The released person is expressing the well-known idea that people do not want to exchange prison for another restrictive facility. The support worker managed to persuade him, but the meeting at this facility was an instant disappointment:

> Entering a facility where there are rules, which is normal—he was afraid of that. But we still went [to the emergency accommodation centre] and the counsellor met us at the entrance. He said "I just got out of prison". The social worker told us he was expected, that she'd put in a word for him. The guy reads the letter and says "What's this? Who are you?". So he says his name: "No, no, no. Nothing has been arranged for you". So you see, apparently everything had been arranged by the social worker, we arrive, no one knows who he is, and the guy throws away the letter from the social worker. I don't know what happened, but while we were waiting the young man looked at me and said "there you go". I was surprised. I told myself that it was the beginning of a long process. It's quite surprising.

The released person and the support worker were facing the challenge of a lack of concrete solutions. In other words, the support rationale was running up against the reality of available housing resources. And the one who was supposed to guide this man's first steps on the outside ended up being put in the position of learning something when the released person showed him what he vaguely knew, calling him to witness ("there you go")—namely that nothing had really been arranged, and that he risked being turned away from the emergency accommodation centre.

However, the moment of release did not mark the end of the relationship. This continued informally and also through the homeless services association that was assisting. It was time to start implementing the plans they had worked out together:

> "I brought him back here since this is where he lives. He saw his buddies again, his friends. I kept in touch with him by phone and in person. I went to see him, sometimes in a place where the homeless congregate, because he himself lived in a squat. So it was going well. Little by little I managed to find him contacts for housing and work, to submit his RSA[182] which was in Toulouse here in the Basque country, and despite all that, all of a sudden bam, he no longer replied. I think he may have felt a bit bullied by the pressure I was putting on him. He no longer kept in touch.

The break was occasioned by a missed appointment which, like in Patrick Declerck's narrative, crystallized the support worker's incomprehension in face of what he perceived as the baffling rejection of a housing solution that was closer than ever:

> What happened was that I arranged a meeting in [city] with an association, so he could be shown a bachelor apartment. It was quite hard to get that far, and to find someone willing to rent him an apartment. The appointment was made for Wednesday at 3pm. The woman went to the appointment but he didn't show up. He didn't give any explanation. She phoned him again, so did I. We left messages, but nothing. I made a few inquiries to find out where he was. He was [at the emergency accommodation centre] where they had ended up finding him something. He told himself: "It's ok, I've found something [at the emergency accommodation centre], it's not worth the trouble to go to [city]". He could have let me know, but he didn't. I don't think

---

182   *Revenu de solidarité active* (a payment that supplements earned income for recipients who are working, or a minimum payment for beneficiaries who are unemployed).

badly of him. But these people are lacking structure, they're certainly lacking tact, and maybe he felt a bit embarrassed, I don't know. He no longer kept in touch.

The support worker found a indirect way to get back in contact, which worked at the time.

One day when I was in [city], [...], I stopped at [the emergency accommodation centre]. He was there but I didn't ask to see him. I didn't want to force my visit on him, so I just left a message saying I wasn't there to monitor or judge him, so he'd feel a little less guilty about putting me in a difficult situation. [...] He phoned two days ago. I told him I was really very happy to hear from him, because I had also been a little worried. Since he was coming off drugs and had unfortunately started drinking—which is typical—alcohol withdrawal was starting too. It's going well. He's very motivated. It's a 36-year-old young man who is really motivated, I think.

Their renewed contact was short-lived and soon broken. The man "no longer kept in touch". The support worker considered it "a little disappointing" at the time. "Maybe he felt that I was hounding him, I don't know". But after being out of touch for a while, they recently got back in contact when the man was admitted to an alcohol detoxification program. Rehabilitation and probation counsellors at another location explained to us that the detoxification treatment offered by regional psychiatric services was viewed unfavourably, because it involved an initial period of voluntary confinement in the facility. People did not want to leave one prison for another. One of these volunteers—a member of the SAMU (an emergency medical service)—thought that the reasons people refused to go to emergency accommodation centres were obvious: loss of privacy, risk of violence, erosion of self-image.

Unthought disciplinary thoughts and psychopathological interpretation

Criticism against Patrick Declerck's analysis centred on his overestimation of the influence of homeless people's psychological pathologies in comparison to the economic and social context of their trajectories. We would like to take this criticism further, shifting it somewhat, by suggesting how difficult it is to offer poor people release conditions that represent a break with both the street and the prison system, in other words how the social lives of homeless people are pervaded by disciplinary mechanisms.

Sociology that deals with homeless people and emergency housing abounds with prison comparisons, if only because many of the people in question have experienced both worlds: "among the underclass, prison [...] is fairly commonplace" (Bruneteaux and Lanzarini 1999). From his immersion in homeless shelters in the 1980s, journalist Jean-Luc Porquet reported the following words from a resident of a shelter in Nancy: "In prison you're treated better than here. Have you seen the food in the canteen? Is it good? It's disgusting! In prison it's better. Here we're lower than dogs. We're here to give them jobs" (Porquet 2007, 28). As Julien Damon explains, as he attempts to historically isolate relatively stable features of the handling of the homeless: "Public policy has always hesitated between security objectives and assistance objectives. Public policy oscillates between repression and solidarity, just as representations of poor and homeless people alternate between hostility and concern for hospitality" (Damon 2003, 26-27).

This is what is shown, for example, by the decades-long biographical itinerary of a homeless man described by Patrick Bruneteaux: "In France until 1994, 'vagabonds' accused of the offence of begging were often forcibly taken to prison, like Georges, who racked up six prison terms, lasting from ten days to a month, between 1968 and 1976" (Bruneteaux 2007, 49). This oscillation has taken a swing in favour of assistance during recent decades. Julien Damon illustrates this "very recent reversal" (Damon 2002, 35) by showing that punishment of the offence of vagrancy decreased during the "Glorious Thirty" (1945-1975), followed by a more drastic shift in the 1960s. From the mid-1980s, less than one hundred convictions were handed down for this offence. By the time the vagrancy law was abolished in 1994, it had largely fallen into disuse. At the same time, from the 1970s, there was an increase in funding allocated for housing benefits (Damon 2002, 37).

However, this trend was not without exceptions, as evinced by "municipal by-laws passed against begging [which] are unquestionably the product of a return to the penalization of poverty, even if the prohibition is no longer provided by penal law, but instead by administrative law" (Damon 2002, 42). As Laurent Bonelli explains, after the first such by-law in 1993, others were passed by mayors of all political stripes (National Front, Communist Party, Socialist Party, the Union for French Democracy, left-wing radicals) (Bonelli 2007a, 43). Fluctuation in the trend was also evinced by urban facilities designed to make the city "deterrent" (Terrolle 2007, 116-117) to the home-less. This "reversal of solidarity with people of no fixed address" is described in terms of the penal deterrence rationale: increase the inconvenience associated with using new urban facilities, so that this outweighs the benefit of having a good location within the city. It expresses well the underlying hostility of this sort of strategy, which, paradoxically, is not confinement but rather—through the impossibility of settling—a manifestation of rejection through invisibilization:

"Thus the initial paradox that traps them seems to be resolved: remaining homeless and on the street without being able to make it their own. Soon there will only be visible transit between the daytime welcome centre or occupational rehabilitation centre, the canteen and the emergency housing centre. Caught in this daily cycle, they will no longer offer visibility testifying to their situation. [...] What is at issue in this development is the declared evasion of poverty and rehabilitation by a political system that, under the pretext of hiding people behind charitable and humanitarian walls or behind those of prisons, will be presented as having permanently resolved the problem of poverty" (Terrolle 2007, 155).

The risk of overestimating the rupture between penal rationalities and rehabilitation rationales also looms over the contrast between the disciplinary function of prisons and the assistance provided by emergency accommodation centres. Of course, living conditions in emergency accommodation centres have not remained unchanged. Reception hours have been extended as a concrete result of mobilization by activists such as "Enfants de Don Quichotte[183]" (Brodiez 2009, 236). But the issue of similarity in how deep poverty is handled in social assistance and penal contexts is part of a longer history. Every winter there are stories in the media about homeless people refusing to go to these centres. This indicates that the lines of opposition between the hostility of prison and the benevolence of solidarity are variable and nuanced. As Patrick Bruneteaux expresses it, "prison methods were set aside, but the uncertainty of how one will be received remains, as part of the rationale of a sphere that is situated in advance of the reintegration sphere. These are places where rights hardly exist, while regulations often take the form of prohibitions and powers of exclusion, which are applied to anyone judged undesirable" (Bruneteaux 2007, 57-58).

A central element that helps explain the prominence of the prison metaphor is the impossibility of controlling one's own schedule. Even if only a partial comparison can be made, life in emergency accommodation centres does entail being deprived of control over time. In fact, "the emergency centres work on the principle of temporary closure. Admission is confinement. Not a major re-confinement, as in the eighteenth century, when people were doomed to working and vegetating in large general hospitals, beggar's jails or prisons. But a

---

183   Literally: Children of Don Quixote

minor, regular confinement. Until morning comes, returning to the street is prohibited. The doors are locked and any movement towards the door sparks a reaction from the staff or the night watchman, who turn them back" (Bruneteaux 2006, 115). Just as new prisons are not putting an end to the suffering associated with confinement, the "prison-like" characteristics of some accommodation facilities are not limited to dilapidation and overcrowding. In one "top-of-the-range" emergency accommodation centre (EAC) operated by the charity *Secours catholique*, there are "rooms for one or two people, a closed changing room operated by a magnetic card. On the other hand, there is no writing table, and hanging things on the walls is prohibited. The beds are bolted to the wall, and people often detached them, which perplexed the staff of this 'modern' EAC. During a discussion organized in the context of a 2002 law on user expression, these professionals discovered that residents could not tolerate a 'bolting' that reminded them of prisons or psychiatric hospitals" (Bruneteaux 2006, 117).

This is also reflected in the account of a released prisoner who registered for training and housing with the help of a volunteer. The housing was modest, but it allowed him to break with the collective world of prison, something that was not possible in shelters:

> "When you hold the key it's different. You come and go when you want, you can go into town. It was a step up in terms of psychological comfort. You don't have any bars, you do what you want, you go where you want. It was too much. And I was alone. It was important for me to be independent right away, instead of being put up in someone else's house and becoming a burden. Even for my family, it wasn't like: 'He's getting out of prison, we have to give him a place to say, what's he going to do?'. Right away I had my own thing, and that allowed me to get on with my plans without bothering people, and make sure it went well. Independence is what matters most. It's not the same as finding yourself in an annoying facility with problem cases.

Even if you're free, it's a continuation. What I have is an opening. It's not finding yourself in the company of someone who's coming out of the closet because he was busted for dope, or an alcoholic, or someone who's depressed, or all of the losers you find in the most miserable places. It wears you out. I found myself surrounded by young people with plans for the future. That's a good thing. It went well right away."

Interview with a former prisoner,
released after a long sentence, 2011.

This distinction was confirmed by the support worker, who had experience with the city's housing organizations through her participation in the mobile emergency medical service for homeless people:

"In the winter when it's very cold, we direct them to shelters, but we do it with a heavy heart. They go into the place, a factory that's been refurbished but it echoes, it's horrible, with white tiles; it's inhuman. And since they mix everyone up, you might have a tramp pissing on you, someone else screaming all night, someone else stealing from you. How can you expect the person to go and sleep there? It would be better to sleep in a park or under a bridge. Entering those places is shocking. Even if there aren't 70 people in the place, it sends shivers down your spine. If I were in the guy's place, I wouldn't go there. You lose your dignity. You have a roof but that's all you have. You have a number."

Interview with a social worker, 2010.

Among the "extreme injuries" to which homeless people are subjected, Corinne Lanzarini described "institutional injuries": treating people like children (managing purchases, a system of punishment and reward, the one-way use of the informal "*tu*" when addressing residents, authorization requests required for anything unplanned), stigmatization (Goffman 1961) ("being subjected to the scrutiny of others to the point that a diffuse, continuous feeling of shame is created" (Lanzarini 2000, 30), the visibility and public nature of assistance, the lack of a sense of ownership of the premises, shared accommodation, the institutional branding of people being admitted, feeling a loss of normality), and institutionally imposed temporalities (opening hours, the duration of assistance, waiting, irregular schedules that result in long, gloomy evenings and expulsion in the small hours). In short, "the underclass's temporality becomes a synthesis of the temporalities of the institutions it frequents, to which is added the travel time between them" (Lanzarini 2000, 34). The conceptual tools designed to describe these institutional injuries suffered by the poorest people are, strikingly, almost the same as those of prison sociology. The comparison could be developed, especially as regards the loss of privacy, not being allowed to choose roommates, conflictual relations with security staff, and sex access problems. This is why "one of the first things ex-prisoners reject is placement in shared accommodation. It is a matter not just of trying to get away from accommodation that reminds them of prison, but of limiting encounters with people they may have met there" (Lanzarini 2000, 31). This analysis is confirmed by a department head at an association that, among other things, manages an emergency accommodation centre for the homeless: "one thing people coming out of prison have difficulty with is finding themselves in a collective context, in the shelter's 'prison without bars'"[184].

This is how volunteers who worked both in prison and with the homeless perceive the continuity of the trajectories of the most vulnerable people:

> "It was always the same people, the same repeat offenders, broken people who got locked up, who emerged at the end of their sentence even more broken, who returned and are now ruined."
> Interview with a volunteer social worker, 2010.

---

184 Interview, 17 September 2009.

"I remember a young homeless person I assisted. He'd been on the streets since he was eight years old. After a while, we found him a place to live. He seems to be doing ok, but even so, there are all kinds of things going on in that place, because he's someone who's always let people take advantage of him. It's the guy who has all the bad luck, who gets bullied from every direction. Even when we managed to get him the RSA, his buddies came along and smashed everything in the apartment, beat him up and stole his money. They know that when he gets his RSA, after eight days there's nothing left.

Interview with the local head of a prison visitor's association, 2010.

The most striking aspect of this description is that it is, in every detail, consistent with the experience of vulnerable people in prison. Even in the context of accommodation that is not in a shelter, and therefore in a regulatory context that has nothing in common with that of places of detention or collective accommodation, the same infringements of space, privacy and financial resources occur. The young man described by the volunteer has only moved out of one prison, into another.

CONCLUSION

"In a world where greatness presupposes displacement, the great draw some of their strength from the immobility of the small, which is the source of the latter's misery. But the least mobile actors are an important factor in the production of the profits the mobile draw from their displacements. In a world where everything displaced itself, the profits generated by displacement, particularly through the coming together of people and worlds that are distant because they are different, would tend to disappear" (Boltanski and Chiapello 2002).

In a book paying tribute to François Bédarida, dedicated to reflections on the idea of writing a history of the present time, Eric Hobsbawm pointed out—not without humour—a fundamental limit to our ability to give an account of events whose aftereffects remain uncertain: "The historian's secret weapon is retrospection. We always win if we bet on horse races that have already finished. But the tragedy of the historian of the present time is precisely that he or she can never go without predicting the future. But prediction has never been historians' strong point" (Hobsbawn 1993, 98). In the same book, Antoine Prost described the history of the present time as "a shaky, rickety, incomplete, unfinished history", but encourages us to "tackle this very incompleteness" instead of "trying to remedy it" (Prost 1993, 359). Caution should be exercised by anyone examining a prison reform whose necessity was publicly debated at the beginning of the 2000s, which was subject to competing elaborations by political, legal and activist actors between 2000 and 2009, which was drafted by the government beginning in 2007 and then finally passed in 2009.

What reform?

In this specific case, if there is any sense in the desire to tackle this incompleteness, it is because what emerges from any examination of the reform process is precisely the uncertainty of its meaning. This uncertainty lies at the conjunction of two simultaneous characterizations of this legislative work: as the recognition of prisoners' rights, or as the restructuring of prison management around the central idea of managing dangerousness and risk. So we will not take the risk of concluding that the reform will lead to this or that certain or probable future, but will instead conclude that the process has not brought an end to public conflict surrounding prisons. Recent demonstrations by guards protesting staff shortages and poor working conditions in spite of their duty of confidentiality[185] have provided a picture of this, illustrating a tenet of the sociology of law creation, according to which "the implementation of a new law provides fuel for future reforms, when actors use it to bring loopholes or limitations to light" (Lévy 2002, 73).

However, beyond these uncertainties, Martine Herzog-Evans, a jurist specializing in penitentiary law and sentence execution law, immediately painted a grim picture of the penitentiary law, which shows just how much disappointment was generated by legislation that should have represented a momentous meeting between France and its prisons. Concerning the general objective of rewriting prison law, she considered that there was "ultimately neither a recodification, nor a restoration of the hierarchy of regulations, other than the legislative elevation of a few of them to the level of established or practically established law" (Herzog-Evans 2010). In other

---

185 Action days were organized on 15 and 22 November 2010. See, for example, *AFP*, "Seconde journée d'action dans la pénitentiaire: nouveaux blocages prévus mercredi", 22 November 2010; *Est-Eclair*, "Contestation interrégionale à Clairvaux", 25 November 2010.

words, the law set forth what was already being practiced, but had been provided by lower-level texts (decrees, circulars, rules); it merely ratified jurisprudential advances resulting from court action that had been taken against the Correctional Service. In the fine details, Martine Herzog-Evans saw modest advances: the formulation of prisoners' right to security, a slight improvement in body search rules, the lowering of the maximum disciplinary wing penalty from 45 to 30 days, the formalization of a pledge of commitment with regard to work, even if this was not an ordinary law contract. In her view, the law also contains a number of regressions: a step backward in terms of rights to information and religious freedom, the introduction of a strange obligation for prisoners to take part in at least one activity (when most prisoners are left with nothing to do because of the CS's inability to offer work or other activities), the increase from one to two years of the sentence remainder that triggers placement in a correctional facility (in other words, the right to keep even more convicts in jails where overpopulation is rife).

It is a meagre result for a legislative undertaking that spanned an entire decade. In the media the law was promptly forgotten, and prisons returned to their usual place in the news, as the object of periodic denouncements for violence, suicide, poor detention conditions, or to celebrate the initiative of an association or prison director. The issue was once again relegated to the margins of public discussion, far removed from the frequent and abundant polemics on miscellany and the incessant desire to toughen penal laws applying to perpetrators of crime. And yet, the Correctional Service Administration has well and truly embraced the reform as an important factor for changing prison management. As the Director of the Correctional Service explained to his troops just after the law was passed by the Assembly, they got what they wanted: "a change of paradigm, and decision-making omnipotence" (Herzog-Evans 2010). This result is all the more surprising for the fact that one of the initial objectives conferred upon the prison reform, specifically by the parliamentary inquiries of 2000, was to limit arbitrariness in prison by restricting the CS's discretionary power. Prison administrators therefore put a lot of effort into imposing their own policy on the reform, in the name of pragmatism, modernization, risk management and risk evaluation.

Neoliberal poverty control: immobilizing, dispossessing, making responsible

A fundamental aspect of this imposition work is the disconnection of prison issues, even though the control tools used for managing the poorest populations circulate between the prison system and the outside world.

The most extreme forms of precarization, as they are described in the United States, for example, by Sébastien Chauvin (Chauvin 2010), show a kind of work management that is characterized much less by work irregularity than by worker immobility. At the "agencies of precariousness" that supply unskilled day labour, candidates applying for a few hours of work must present themselves at 4:30 am, get their names registered as high as possible on the list of arrivals and then wait, without any guarantee of results (since the list order is quite often ignored for the sake of arbitrary choices based on personal preference or the desire to punish). Successful candidates must be placed on a work "ticket", board a bus that drops workers at various factories, work, wait for the return bus to arrive, and then go home. One person Chauvin met said he only had time to sleep four hours per night. Chauvin described the agency's "detention centre" atmosphere, the complete loss of control over time this organization induced, factories that operated like "suburban prisons" (Chauvin 2010, 152, 156) that are impossible to leave because of their distance from the city centre, the deep sense of arbitrariness some people can feel depending on whether or not they are hired for day labour, the impossibility of complaining and the need to keep tirelessly returning to show an acceptable attitude. Even the furnished hotel for poor workers was more like a supervisory authority (same schedules, same people) than a commercial service, and the drivers of the long-distance bus lines used by people who lacked the means to fly behaved more like prison guards than service providers (Chauvin 2010, 325). Forced immobility is obviously the primary aspect of prison punishment—spatial punishment *par excellence*—but immobility, uncertainty and arbitrariness are a part of the everyday lives not just of prisoners, but also of workers exploited by a neoliberal economy.

Another feature of the change in how the state manages poverty is described as the "activation" of social expenditure—in other words, the rulers' desire to reduce the amount of assistance distributed unconditionally in favour of payments received on condition of activity (work, training, education, etc.). To express it in terms of the American context, it is a shift from the *welfare state* to the *workfare state*. In France, even if it does not boil down to this, it is a rationale that has been put forward to advocate the passing of laws on the RMI[186] and the RSA[187] (Méda 2008). The RMI is the minimum revenue paid to people over the age of twenty-five who no longer have the right to ordinary social protection revenue (like unemployment benefits). The RSA provides a partial social welfare payment if part-time work has been resumed, so that this resumption does not end up resulting in no overall gain for the beneficiary of the allowance. Therefore, compared to the RMI, the RSA functions independently as supplementary earnings, a hybrid between the maintenance of the social safety net and a reconfiguration that encourages beneficiaries to work, a formula that can be supported by MPs on the left as well as on the right.

The desire to "activate" prisoners presents a paradoxical situation. On the one hand, it seems to come naturally to right-wing political leaders, who included an "activity obligation" in the penitentiary reform. On the other hand, it presents two problems. Firstly, it would seem to amount to a partial return to the old days when convicts were forced to work, a disciplinary imperative inherited

---

186   *Revenu minimum d'insertion.*
187   *Revenu de solidarité active.*

from 19th-century prisons that was abolished in 1980. In this sense, it would be particularly tricky to implement because the refusal to work would have to be subject to disciplinary sanctions, whose legitimacy would be rather flimsy. Secondly, and perhaps more fundamentally, the prison context exacerbates the contradiction on the outside between the desire to impose work and the lack of available jobs. Work, as well as cultural, educational and training activities, depend on several actors: the Correctional Service, the companies operating in prisons, and the associations involved with prisons. But these do not depend on the desires of prisoners. The lack of activity, especially work activity, in a context of substantial unemployment, underlines the structural limitations of any desire for activation based on encouraging prisoners.

This remark holds true more generally for another notion transposed into the penal vocabulary, a central notion expressing transformations in the state's modes of operation: the *plan*. The Correctional Service introduced this notion through the term Sentence Execution Plan (SEP), based on the idea of ending up with a kind of blueprint or unwritten contract with a convict that establishes the different stages of detention. In the outside world, sociologists have shown that there is something artificial about encouraging benefits recipients to devise reintegration plans, when it is unlikely that the poorest among them will find stable employment on the job market. Formalizing the plan is reduced to a rhetorical condition defining an acceptable beneficiary, without any illusions about its chances of being realized.

Expert opinion about release from prison is caught between the formalization of risk evaluation and the realization that this evaluation runs up against the most stubborn fact of release from prison, namely (significant) social precariousness. Those who promote approaching probation through desistance believe that "desistance can, it seems, be provoked by someone believing in the offender; someone who perhaps carries hope and keeps it alive when the offender cannot do so for him or herself. Of course, the brutal reality is that the social circumstances of the lives of many repeat offenders suffocate hope" (McNeill and Weaver 2010, 17). Or to put it more bluntly, "hope, expectation and confidence fade quickly on an empty stomach" (McNeill et Weaver 2010, 7).

In a prison context, these plans, which are defined with a semblance of autonomy and dialogue, are plainly overdetermined by the length of sentences, just as they are likely to be reconsidered following incidents subject to discipline, or might change according to the vagaries of work and training opportunities. If we take seriously the reality that sentences are supposed to impose suffering, we see that it is illogical to ask someone who is doomed to a certain quantity of suffering to choose the moment when this will be turned into a vehicle of positive change. As with "activity", transposing the "plan" notion into the prison context provides the observer with a magnifying glass revealing the deceptive nature of the individualization of the fight against poverty and social precariousness—all the more when it is part of a disciplinary context. Plan formulation becomes an objective that can be neither realized nor abandoned. This also sheds light on the punitive, moralizing rationality at work when social security is granted with conditions. This aspect was particularly visible when the Right tried several times to legislate the suspension of family allowance benefits in cases where the children in the family no longer attend school and/or commit criminal acts.

Those with the least means to take responsibility and control over their lives are also those who are the most subjected to this injunction. Prison, the last stop on a journey of exclusion, presents this process in a polished, wrapped up form, in which the socially imposed demand to behave like an autonomous, free and enterprising individual becomes a heavy burden on individuals who lack the conditions to act (Chantraine 2004; Chantraine and Mary 2006).

Social order and critical challenges

The challenge is to grasp the connection between the unique perspective of inmates with its political dimension and efforts to sociologically objectify prison's relationship to the structure of the social order. At the beginning of Luc Boltanski's book about forms of critique (Boltanski 2011), he analyzes the difference between the critical sociology of domination and the pragmatic sociology of critique. The former, associated with the work of Pierre Bourdieu, analyzes the position of individuals within the social order, and derives hierarchies, powers and instances of symbolic violence from a more general state of domination, a state whose revelation is unique to sociology, particularly because the actors themselves are "sunk in illusion" (Boltanski 2009, 23). The pragmatic sociology of critique, associated with the work of Boltanski among others, considers that the sociology of domination subjects the uniqueness of the world to an oversimplification based on an overly univocal domination model, and is for that reason little able to explain the concrete forms of social critique in which the actors themselves engage. It is therefore necessary to base social criticism not just on a sociological discourse that reveals the social order, but also on the *"point of view of actors* - that is to say, base itself on their moral sense and, in particular, on their ordinary sense of justice, to expose the discrepancy between the social world as it is and as it should be in order to satisfy people's moral expectations." (Boltanski 2009, 30).

Luc Boltanski recognizes that the tendency of the pragmatic sociology of critique to emphasize the critical abilities of individual actors is linked to the context of its development, that is, to "a moment of history characterized by the defeat of attempts made in previous decades to validate a collective conception of justice, conceived as social justice." (Boltanski 2009, 32). In other words, forms of protest, and their detachment from the critique of an unjust social order are themselves linked to the political situation, and to the abilities of collective organizations to mount challenges. The range of potential protesters varies according to the ability of actors to provide a "sense of totality, opening up the possibility of moving back-and-forth between the particular situations of which actors have direct experience and the wider social orders that can only be accessed through the mediation of political constructs" (Boltanski 2009, 33-34). This is why the "self-restriction of protests is [...] at its greatest in atomized social situations where individuals can only rely on their own forces, and it diminishes in periods when collective action seems possible and, in particular, in exceptional situations—revolutionary or insurrectional" (Boltanski 2009, 35).

From this perspective, the 1970s marked a decisive turning point. Contrary to a critical view that describes the period of the postwar social struggles as a golden age, one must acknowledge the extent to which political organizations that existed prior to May 1968 disregarded prison issues, just as they disregarded gender issues. Nevertheless, the specialization of forms of critique, caught in the activism ebb of the late 1970s, must be questioned to consider new links between minority challenges and challenges to the social order.

Among the tests that institutions must undergo, Luc Boltanski designates the most radical as an *existential test*: "at least when it ends up being formulated and made public, it unmasks the *incompleteness* of reality and even its *contingency*, by drawing examples from the flux of life that make its bases unstable and challenge it, in such a way as to confront it with the inexhaustible, and hence impossible to *totalize*, reserve represented by *the world*" (Boltanski 2011, 113). An existential test is distinct from a *truth test*, a way of justifying the institution through itself. In the field of social criticism, it is also distinct from a *reality test*, by means of which the institution is held to its word by its detractors, for example to show that it failed to do what it said it would do, or that it is not achieving the results that are supposed to legitimize its existence. The penal system, and specifically prison, lends itself to this type of criticism, which has been thoroughly developed in an effort to show that, although prison is an institution that imposes legal penalties, it operates outside of any sense of ordinary law, that although prison must encourage rehabilitation it engenders desocialization, that penal severity does not reduce crime. The abundance of opportunities to express this sort of criticism shows the contrast with other ways of repudiating penality that, to use Stéphane Legrand's words, attempt "to conceive an original connection between the universal and the local or, to express it better, between micropolitical strategies proper to power's small networks and the macropolitical issues of the social struggle as a whole" (Legrand 2007).

What is difficult for individuals condemned to immobility and to making plans that their position in the economic and social world doom to failure, is to get people to hear another story about their condition, different from the one about being stigmatized as abnormal, maladjusted and dangerous. And yet these alternative stories could be boosted by extending the critical analysis of prisons to their handling of the most vulnerable people. For Loïc Wacquant, the scientific objectification of the "organic link between social justice and criminal justice" should enlighten civil society on the need to break the silos between their respective struggles. According to Wacquant: "It is essential to *forge connections between activists and researchers on the penal and social fronts,* between members of unions and associations in the welfare, education, housing, and health sectors, on the one hand, and their counterparts mobilized around the police, justice, and correctional services, on the other" (Wacquant, 2009, 286). In our view, one essential connection is the link between prison issues and problems with employment, housing and health. This could be highlighted by focusing on conflicts between the actors that define official penal system discourse and those who are attempting to draw attention to the gap between this discourse and their own experiences. In other words, the thinking behind the present text was rooted in the conviction that a willingness to "go and listen" to the points of view of the most disadvantaged prisoners can enable researchers to make important observations that can be useful for understanding and criticizing the operation of the contemporary penal system. In this sense, scientific research must show just as much interest in identifying macro-sociological mechanisms that reconfigure the relationships of domination between social groups as it does in circulation, transfers and the translation of social forms of criticism.

Scanty publicization of prisoners' experiences and grievances is part of a long history. As Michelle Perrot explains, "there have always been protest movements in prisons" (Perrot 2004), but "nothing too precise that attains the dignity of an event", "rather a vague background noise, a muted rumour, distant, perhaps extinguishing, without our knowing whether this silence should be attributed to the strength of the walls, resignation on the inside, or indifference on the outside" (Perrot 1975, 70). The extent of the prison system's isolation has of course changed a great deal since the mid-nineteenth century, when a prison revolt causing deaths in Embrun could be completely denied by administration managers (Perrot 1980, 279). Nonetheless, beyond prison's openness to external organizations and the facilitation of information transmission, the struggle to give a politically audible voice to prisoners and the most socially vulnerable people, "fenced in by contempt, the highest of all walls" (Perrot 1975, 87), remains highly relevant.

EPILOGUE
The Great Escape - France and Its Prisons in 2112

"Come! Come quickly sir! One of them is missing! Someone's escaped!"

Mr Martin, the old head guard, ran to join guards Suret and Coute at the door of Cell 317. As required by regulations, he had already activated his alarm and all of the guards in the building were rushing to the scene.

"Look sir, there's a head made of cardboard, so we'd think he was there during night rounds."

Martin popped his head into the cell and saw the subterfuge.

"The little bastard! And he does this the day before my retirement!"

More guards were starting to arrive, and a small, excited crowd was trying to squeeze into the cell. Suret and Coute thought maybe their joke was getting a little out of hand so they owned up to the prank:

"Come on guys, it's just a joke! The last prisoner on this level was released this morning. Since the boss didn't know, we decided to surprise him!"

The others walked away grumbling. Obviously an escape was not something that delighted them, but during that summer of 2112, enthusiasm was seriously lacking at Mont-de-Marsan prison.

It was a large complex inherited from the era of rising prison populations a century earlier. After being privatized it had quickly fallen into disrepair. For decades, it had been slowly emptying of prisoners. Originally designed for 700 people, it had housed up to 1,100 prisoners, before following the trend of decline that would most likely lead to permanent closure by the end of the year. A small building with thirty places had been opened closer to the city centre. There were around twenty prisoners left, all awaiting transfer or release. No one would have had the preposterous idea to plan an escape. The guards were bored stiff, especially Suret (nick-named Big Head) who killed time pulling pranks.

Only this time, he may have gone a little too far. When Martin had pulled alarm, it had automatically alerted the prefect and the prosecutor. Even a reporter from the local rag appeared at the entrance looking for information. Mr Neullety, the prison director, had been forced to tell a lie to calm everyone down—about a technical malfunction—and had been furious.

So Coute was feeling uneasy the next morning as he climbed the stairs to Neullety's office. Suret was calmer, and this exasperated Coute.

"Don't you realize we're in for the biggest dressing down of our lives?"

"Don't worry," Suret answered. "I've been through this before. You just have to weather the storm and then wait for the right moment to bring up the carceral population reduction policy and the 'Brussels Plan' or whatever it's called."

The prison director was just coming out of his office, and he heard Suret's last words.

"Come on Suret, it's not the "Brussels Plan", it's the "Amsterdam Plan". How can you confuse them? Don't you know how they got those names?"

"No sir," the guard said, delighted to see that the director was already forgetting the reason for their visit.

"It was in 2077, thirty-five years ago, when the penal policy had hit rock bottom. In this very prison, there were bunk beds, mattresses on the floor and lots of violence. This was the case all over Europe. No one knew yet, but they were approaching the end of almost continual carceral population increases, on the same model as the 1975-2010 increases, except for the fact that they started with higher numbers: 75,000 prisoners in 2030, 120,000 at the start of my career. In 1970, there were 6 prisoners per 10,000 inhabitants. At the turn of the 21st century, that figure had risen to 10 per 10,000. By the end of the century it was up to 20 per 10,000. I watched this happening from my office in the Correctional Service Administration. I'd been hired as PA to the director, Bernard Colvin. Day after day I listened to him cursing the Ministry of Justice, which couldn't go six months without proposing a new penal reform. I couldn't stand listening to it anymore. Suddenly I mustered some courage and made a comment with consequences I could never have imagined"

I said: 'Sir, don't you think we could try to do something about it?'

He thought for a moment, and then said:

'Look, I'm two years from retirement. I can always try to do something in my little corner. We can't make decisions for the government, but we can at least try to enlighten it. What's been lacking most in recent years is a concrete demonstration that we could do things differently. And do you know where we could find everything we need to show them?'

Obviously I said no.

'At the library. Now that all of Europe has adopted the same idiotic policies, we've lost sight of the idea that we could do something completely different. We need to find documented alternative experiences. You'll spend six months at the National Library of France.'

I was not very enthusiastic. It was to escape that library that I had abandoned my thesis and taken a job at the Ministry of Justice. I tried to get out of it.

'Sir, as you know, all of my work days have to be justified to the Finance Ministry. What are we going to tell them?'

With a little smile, he said:

'We'll call your mission *Amsterdam*. You can double-check this, but I'm almost sure that Holland is one country that went to great lengths to avoid the use of prison. We'll tell the Ministry of Justice that you've been given the task of writing a report on the Improvement of the National Strategic Research Mission for More Dynamic Facilities and Methods. They'll like that. It's settled. You start tomorrow. Send me a brief weekly report.'

He went back to his office, saying in a singsong voice: 'There you go, I've launched my little Amsterdam.'

Mr. Neullety had recounted this conversation as if it had taken place only the day before, but this memory made him pensive. Suret worried that this silence would give him the chance to remember what he and Coute were doing there. Even though he already knew the broad outline of the story, Suret asked:

"But what was in the report?"

"Lots of things!" Neullety continued. "For example, at the time, long sentences were continually extended, particularly because of so-called security periods, the minimum time that had to be served without any chance of having your sentence reduced. We took these periods so much for granted that we no longer asked ourselves where they'd come from. In fact, in history books I discovered that they hadn't been around very long. They didn't exist at all before 1978[188], and when this law was passed, the Left was against it! At the time of my report, we had reached the point of handing down bona fide life sentences based on the American model, without any possibility of release, whereas in 1960 and 1970 the average time served under a life sentence was 17 years (Barré and Tournier 1982). Today that seems like an eternity, but at the time, to say that everyone should get out someday ran counter to a strong trend (Kensey 2005). It was treated like a revolutionary proposal!"

"Is that why the number of prisoners increased?"

"In part, yes. Taking a fresh look at the numbers, I noticed that this was how the carceral population increase had begun, starting in 1980, by increasing the length of sentences (Aubusson de Cavarlay 2005). Then this trend was exacerbated by flow increases (Aubusson de Cavarlay

---

188   Law no. 78-1097 of 22 November 1978 changing certain provisions of the Code of Criminal Procedure relating to the execution of custodial sentences.

2008), which I couldn't really understand. Sometimes the numbers would go up without any change in the law. I had to read newspapers from that time to understand the reason for it: if a crime-related news item was trumpeted by the press and the government, this was enough to spark sudden increases in the number of people sent to prison (Tournier 2011c)!"

"How strange!"

"Another strange thing was that at the time, the solution was not all that difficult to find. When I was starting the 'Amsterdam report', all neighbouring countries were in agreement about the prison tryptic of uncertainty / penal severity / privatization (Christie 2003). But a century earlier, one could read numerous critical studies of the penal system (Christie 1981, Hulsmann and Bernat de Celis, 1982, Mathiesen 2006 [1990], Davis 2003, Larsen and Piché 2010) and follow nearby examples, such as Finland, which had gone from having one of the highest incarceration rates in Europe (187 per 100,000 in the 1950s) to having one of the lowest (55 prisoners per 100,000 habitants in 2000) (Lappi-Seppälä 2005)."

Marc Neullety had stood up. He continued his story looking out the window, as if he were addressing a large auditorium.

"Do you think he even remembers we're here?" whispered Coute, now less worried.

Suret, who wanted to know more, signalled for him to be quiet.

"Within France itself," the director continued, "several reports existed that explained how to achieve this (CNCDH 2007b): reduce maximum sentences, expand the use of early, assisted releases, strictly limit the use of pre-trial detention, develop effective alternatives like community service and, above all, stay the course. The same went for prisons: the European experts concurred, saying that countries shouldn't be increasing the number of prisons to keep up with the prison population rise (Conseil de l'Europe 1999). Inspection reports clearly showed that hastily built large prisons were ticking time bombs (Contrôleur général des lieux de privation de liberté 2009)."

"Why didn't anyone react?"

"That's what it took me a long time to understand. In France, there were brief periods when things moved in the right direction, in the early 1980s and at the turn of the 21st century for example. But every time, the government that had implemented these guidelines would change them before leaving office, and then the increase would resume. I started to better understand why this was the case when I saw how people spoke about penal issues. At the time, the Minister of the Interior could come along and say, just by reading police statistics, that crime had decreased by 2.3% in such and such month, not 2.2 or 2.4. I'm not exaggerating, it was down to a tenth of a percentage point."

"They spoke of 'crime' in general?" Suret exclaimed. "They added up murders and the most minor offenses in the same calculation? They though that police figures corresponded to crime in the real world? But that doesn't make any sense (Robert 1977)!"

"Obviously not. Also, there were plenty of people ready to point this out every time (Mucchielli 2011a). But it didn't do any good. Every once in a while, the minister would declare that we needed to start fighting the crimes of nationals from this or that country and presto!... these crimes would increase in the police statistics (Mucchielli 2011b). I happened to be reading an article on Jacques Mesrine—a longtime crook who made headlines more than a century ago—just when the government started talking about public "security" every day, and I understood that "the day has come when people are so fed up with crime that they accept not knowing what is happening in the realm of a justice being dispensed in their name" (Foucault 1977). So I stated in my "Amsterdam report" that an even more urgent task than technical incarceration reduction measures was to try and change how we talked about these issues. This is how we were able to raise the issue of decriminalizing drugs (Coppel 2010), and to show that, for young offenders, the less they were stigmatized by the justice system, the greater their chances of getting out of it later (McNeill and Weaver 2010). At first, no one believed it, but more and more examples came to light. There were even American states that had abolished prisons for minors in the 1960s[189]."

Mr Neullety became lost in thought for a moment, and then continued:

"That's the reason why my boss had sent me to the library: he wanted a sample group of alternatives that had worked. And I ended up finding what he wanted: the imprisonment rate Holland had achieved, 18 people per 100,000 inhabitants in 1973 (Brodeur 2006), five times less than that of France in the 2000-2010 period, forty times less than the United States in 2010. This became the guiding line of my report: since it had existed, it certainly had to be possible to reproduce it. But how was it to be done? We tried to establish a roadmap, explaining that the most important thing was to keep our discourse consistent, and do so over quite a long period. Basically, we explained to the minister that he must stop doing what had more or less been his only idea: taking advantage of every sensational news item in order to push through repressive laws that were often disastrous or unenforceable (Bourdieu 2002)."

"So your report wasn't implemented right away?"

"Certainly not! At first, it was put in a drawer. But a short time later, in the early 2080s, a new majority came to power. The minister's principal private secretary called me to his office. He was of two minds. He was afraid of drawing the ire of the critics and scuttling the government's popularity. It's true that in the report, in order to explain the failure of past initiatives, I had clearly shown that political leaders who wanted to limit the use of prison found themselves caught up in fierce controversies. The secretary reminded me of the example of an American state governor in the 1980s, a presidential candidate, whose campaign was

---

189   "Massachusetts has had no youth prisons in operation since 1972" Dennie Briggs wrote in 1975, in (Briggs 1975) *In Place of Prison*, London, Morris Temple Smith, 1975, p. 63.

ruined by the recidivism of a criminal he had decided to release (Lamalice and Lalande 2006; Anderson 1995). And since his minister had certain ambitions... Over a period of two hours, I explained that all of the proposed measures had had encouraging results in terms of recidivism prevention. But I concluded by throwing out: 'Ultimately, it doesn't only depend on you'."

"What did you mean?"

"From what I was able to read, the relations between penal issues and broader social issues had long been the subject of academic debate[190], but it seemed quite clear to me that, to address penal problems differently, it was first necessary to stop viewing them as central. This was what I had retained from the formula of a sociologist I hadn't understood at first: during the growth period that followed the Second World War, crime wasn't considered a major social phenomenon, but rather a residual phenomenon, bound to decrease as a result of social progress (Robert 2002)."

"Obviously!" Suret exclaimed.

"It seems obvious to us now, but at the time of the "Amsterdam report", and for a long time before, there had been a major social crisis. One of the consequences was that the government was constantly explaining that crimes were increasingly serious, more and more violent, and perpetrated by younger and younger people. This was far from having been proven (Mucchielli 2008a), but, at the same time, given the nature of the political leaders' rhetoric, it was difficult to get people to hear quite another story—for example, the fact that the number of homicides was not on the rise (Mucchielli 2008b)! The principal private secretary said: 'We'll do what we can.' This meant: resurrecting a policy of supporting crime prevention associations, increasing the number social workers in prison, making a bit of funding available for community work. It was better than nothing, but it was very

---

190   For example, Georg Rusche and Otto Kirschheimer, *Punishment and Social Structure*, New York, Colombia University Press, 1939; Charlotte Vanneste, *Les chiffres des prisons, des logiques économiques à leur traduction pénale*, Paris, L'Harmattan, 2001; Loïc Wacquant, *Punishing the Poor: The Neoliberal Government of Social Insecurity*, Duke University Press, 2009.

flimsy, and it didn't change much for prisoners serving long sentences. This is how things stood for a few years."

"And after that was June 2083?"

"That changed everything. It all started with small protests by a few marginal groups. No one ever imagined it would grow so big! And it's true that these were the years when it started becoming possible to discuss things seriously. The first important decision was to refer every matter to the collegial commission dealing with the issue presented by the infraction. This is how we were able to start making advances: gradually withdrawing drugs issues and all immigration issues from the Penal Code, but also setting precise targets for the use of social rehabilitation options for all of the poor people, minors and young adults who were continually in and out of prison (Chantraine 2004; Bruneteaux Lanzarini 1999). It took some time and there were failures, but one of the lessons people had retained from previous experiences was that steadfastness was essential."

"Did it happen gradually?" asked Coute, who had finally decided to show interest in the conversation, even if it meant getting stuck in the director's office.

"No. There were clashes and disagreements, mainly over two points. The first was resolved fairly quickly. The new leaders wanted to tackle financial illegalities, and I must admit that all studies showed that they were rarely pursued, that the criminals convicted were rarely the most important ones and that those responsible rarely spent much time behind bars (Lascoumes 1997). Convicted politicians were even sometimes re-elected and this intrigued researchers (Lascoumes 2010). The new leaders wanted to change tack somewhat, wishing to enact laws that would make it so that sentences were based on how much money the state was deprived of as a result of the various frauds, and on how many lives could have been improved, even saved, with this money. With this method, beyond a few million, we would have reached sentences equal to those for homicide! For a few months, having a few dozen white collar criminals in jail made everyone happy. But, quite quickly, what was considered central was financial regulation and taxation, and financial criminals started benefitting from the same penal regime as the one for scooter thieves, which was itself improving! This is also when we entered another development model. All of this started to interest people much more than the fate of the hoodlums of yesteryear."

"So everything was resolved easily?"

"No. What was really difficult and complicated was the issue of violence, especially sexual violence."

"Why?"

"We were in a difficult situation. Since the 1970s, there had been major protests, an increase in the number of formal complaints, and people were being given longer sentences for sex crimes (Burricand, Monteil 1996). There were quite a few legislative changes, and it was in the name of the fight against repeat sexual offenses that the harshest measures were introduced: unconditional detention periods, post-release electronic bracelets[191], security retention which made it possible to keep people locked up indefinitely after their initial sentence[192], criminal files[193] and, beginning in 2020, something we had copied from the United States: posting the photos, addresses and criminal records of released sexual offenders online[194]."

"That's horrifying!" exclaimed Coute, who had forgotten it was lunchtime. "But did these policies have results?"

"The irony, which was described by inquiries conducted at the turn of the 21st century (Jaspard 2005; Bajos, Bozon et al. 2008), is that the number of formal complaints lodged remained very small in relation to the statements of individuals at victim inquiries. This is why the heads of the inquiries explained that 'repression was often a simplistic,

---

191   Law no. 2005-1549 of 12 December 2005 relating to the handling of repeat criminal offences.

192   Law no. 2008-174 of 25 February 2008 relating to security retention and the declaration of diminished responsibility due to mental illness.

193   Like the automatic judicial database of sexual or violent offenders (FIJAIS - le fichier judiciaire automatisé des auteurs d'infractions sexuelles ou violentes), created by the Perben II law of 9 March 2004.

194   National Sex Offender Public Website or at the state level, Florida Sexual Offenders and Predators.

even demagogical response to the anxiety and fear often orchestrated to turn attention away from socio-political problems' and that 'what was really needed was a social solution to the phenomenon that was not limited to penal sanctions, but also included prevention and victim assistance' (Jaspard 2005, 105). The problem was 'to break the wall of silence that paralyzes victims'."

"Do you mean that most people didn't tell anyone about what had happened to them?"

"Yes. Well, in any case, they didn't tell the police and no legal action was taken. What changed significantly in the late 2080s was that people spoke much more openly as a large number of activist groups was created. There was a sudden increase in the number of complaints lodged, and it was very clear that this was going to lead to a major increase in the carceral population. Meetings were organized between the "Penal Justice" and "Violence" subcommittees, and it was quite a slinging match! At first, I thought I had the lethal weapon. Ever since writing the "Amsterdam report", I had continued going to the library and I had read all of the feminist texts that explained why prison was not an effective solution[195]. But it was complicated: for example, how were victims of domestic violence to be protected without imprisoning the perpetrator, or at least tracking his movements through an electronic bracelet?[196] After a while, they were going in circles and they stopped the meetings."

"How was it settled?"

"It's hard to say. In fact, I believe things changed when the inquiries showed that, due to everything that had been implemented elsewhere, incidents of violence were decreasing significantly. Attention was concentrated on prevention and mediation policies, on work and housing and so on, and penal measures fell into disuse. It was at this time that the abrogation laws were passed: life sentences, unconditional detention periods, electronic bracelets, criminal

---

195   On these debates, see Jean Bérard's thesis (Bérard 2013).
196   Law no. 2010-769 of 9 July 2010 relating to violence specifically against women, violence between couples and violence against children.

files and security retention. At that time, I was an advisor to the Minister of Justice; I wrote his speeches. When the law abrogating security retention was being passed, I thought I was working on a historic text. Several times I had listened to Badinter's speech on the abolition of the death penalty. And in fact it was passed on the sly, in the middle of the night, by a handful of deputies... Later, I still had a little moment of pleasure: when we started getting close to the "Amsterdam 1973" imprisonment rate, I convinced the minister to make a speech. At a welcome ceremony for a new class at the National Centre for Judicial Studies, the Minister began his speech with these words: "Just as the right to life denies the death penalty, the right to freedom will sooner or later lead to the condemnation of custodial sentences. We're not there yet, but the path has been laid...". The minister was very happy with me. I didn't dare confess that this wording also came from my trips to the library (Tulkens 2001, 281)... Anyway, why am I tell you all this? Suret, Coute, clear off and no more jokes!"

Going back down the stairs, Suret was a little shaken:

"There's no future in the Correctional Service. I think I'll try to find research work. You know, rummaging through archives, finding evidence. This whole Amsterdam story... There must be lots of documents, and people who were there and lived it. I'm wondering if what the boss told us is true. I really want to know."

"Do they pay people to do that?"

"I don't know."

BIBLIOGRAPHY

Administration pénitentiaire. 2008. *Chiffres clefs 2007 - Perspectives 2008*. Paris: Direction de l'administration pénitentiaire.

Anderson, David. 1995. *Crime and the Politics of Hysteria. How the Willie Horton Story Changed American Justice*. New York:Random House.

Armazet, André. 1973. *Tout savoir sur les prisons*. Paris: Filipacchi.

Artières, Philippe, Lascoumes, Pierre, and Grégory Salle. 2004. "Gouverner et enfermer. La prison, un modèle indépassable ?." In *Gouverner et enfermer. La prison, un modèle indépassable*, edited by Philippe Artières, Pierre Lascoumes and Grégory Salle, 23-51. Paris: Presses de Sciences Po.

Artières, Philippe, Quéro, Laurent, and Michelle Zancarini-Fournel. 2003. "Contexte." In *Groupe d'information sur les prisons, archives d'une lutte, 1970-1972*, edited by Philippe Artières, Laurent Quéro and Michelle Zancarini-Fournel, 13-19. Paris : Editions de l'IMEC.

Aubusson de Cavarlay, Bruno. 1985. "Hommes, peines et infractions, la légalité de l'inégalité." *L'Année sociologique* 3/35:275-309.

Aubusson de Cavarlay, Bruno. 2005. "Police de rue, justice d'urgence." *Dedans dehors* 47: 18-19.

Aubusson de Cavarlay, Bruno. 2007. "Risques calculés." In *Politiques du risque*, edited by Gilles Chantraine. *Vacarme* 40: http://www.vacarme.org/article1327.html.

Aubusson de Cavarlay, Bruno. 2008. "La nouvelle inflation carcérale." In *La frénésie sécuritaire. Retour à l'ordre et nouveau contrôle social*, edited by Laurent Mucchielli, 52-63. Paris: La Découverte.

Audier, Serge. 2008. *La pensée anti-68, essai sur les origines d'une restauration intellectuelle*. Paris: La Découverte.

Bajos, Nathalie, Bozon, Michel *et al.* 2008. "Les violences sexuelles en France, quand la parole se libère." *Population et société* 445:1-4.

Barker, Vanessa. 2009. *The Politics of Imprisonment: How the Democratic Process Shapes the Way America Punishes Offenders*. New York: Oxford University Press.

Badinter, Robert. 1992. *La prison républicaine, 1871-1914*. Paris:Fayard.

Barré, Marie-Danièle, and Pierre-Victor Tournier 1982. "Érosion des peines perpétuelles. Analyse des cohortes des condamnés à mort graciés et des condamnés à une peine perpétuelle libérés entre le 1er janvier 1961 et le 31 décembre 1980." *Travaux et Documents* 16.

Bastard, Benoît, Mouhanna, Christian and Werner Ackermann. 2005. *Une justice dans l'urgence. Le traitement en temps réel des affaires pénales.* Paris : GIP Droit et Justice.

Bauman, Zygmunt. 2000. "Social Uses of Law and Order." In *Criminology and Social Theory*, edited by David Garland and Richard Sparks, 23-46. Oxford: Oxford University Press.

Beck, Ulrich. 1992. *Risk Society. Towards a New Modernity.* London: Sage.

Becker, Howard. 1966. *Outsiders: Studies in the Sociology of Deviance.* New York: Free Press.

Becker, Howard. 1967. "Whose Side Are We On?" *Social Problems* 14: 239–47.

Bérard, Jean and Hugues de Suremain. 2009. "La gestion des longues peines au révélateur des luttes juridiques." *Champ pénal / Penal field* 6: http://champpenal.revues.org/7698.

Bérard, Jean, and Stéphanie Coye. 2005. "Sécurité renforcée en prison : la fabrique de violences." *Dedans-dehors* 49:9-11.

Bérard, Jean. 2010. "Libérer des détenus, libéraliser les prisons ? Révoltes des prisonniers et réformes pénitentiaires (1968-1975)." In *1968 entre libération et libéralisation*, edited by Michel Margairaz and Danièle Tartakowsky, 183-200. Rennes: Presses Universitaires de Rennes.

Bérard, Jean. 2011. *Sortir et s'en sortir, Pauvreté des prisonniers, aménagement des peines de prison, innovation pénale.* Rapport de recherche. Lille : CLERSE.

Bérard, Jean. 2013. *La justice en procès. Les mouvements de contestation face au système pénal (1968-1983).* Paris: Presses de Sciences-po.

Bishop, Norman. 2006. "La participation des personnes détenues à l'organisation de la vie en détention." *Champ Pénal / Penal Field* 3:http://champpenal.revues.org/document485.html.

Boltanski Luc and Eve Chiapello, 2002. "Inégaux face à la mobilité." *Projet* 271: http://www.ceras-projet.org/index.php?id=1796.

Boltanski, Luc and Laurent Thévenot. 2006. *On Justification : Economies of Worth.* Princeton: Princeton University Press.

Boltanski, Luc. 2009. *De la critique, précis de sociologie de l'émancipation.* Paris: Gallimard.

Bonelli, Laurent. 2007a. *La France a peur, une histoire sociale de " l'insécurité ".* Paris: La Découverte.

Bonelli, Laurent. 2007b. "Policing the youth : towards a redefinition of discipline and social control in French working-class neighbourhoods." In Y*outh, Globalization and the Law*, edited by Sudhir Venkatesh, 90-123. Stanford: Stanford University Press.

Bourdieu Pierre. 1994. "L'emprise du journalisme." *Actes de la recherche en sciences sociales* 101-102:102-109.

Bourdieu, Pierre *et al*. 1999. *Weight of The World: Social Suffering in Contemporary Society*. Oxford: Polity Press.

Bourdieu, Pierre. 1986. "La force du droit, éléments pour une sociologie du champ juridique." *Actes de la recherche en sciences sociales* 1/64:3-19.

Bourdieu, Pierre. 2000. *Pascalian Meditations*. New York: Polity Press.

Briggs, Dennie. 1975. *In place of prison*. London: Morris Temple Smith.

Brodeur, Jean-Paul. 2006. "Comparative Penology in Perspective." In *Crime and Justice. An Annual Review of Research*, edited by Michael Tonry, 49-91. Chicago: Chicago University Press.

Brodeur, Jean-Paul. 2007. "De grandes espérances." *Criminologie* 40/2:161-166.

Brodiez, Axelle. 2009. *Emmaüs et l'abbé Pierre*. Paris: Presses de Sciences-po.

Brossat, Alain. 2001. *Pour en finir avec la prison*. Paris: La Fabrique.

Brunet-Ludet, Cécile. 2010. *Le droit d'expression collective des personnes détenues*. Paris: Direction de l'administration pénitentiaire.

Bruneteaux, Patrick and Corinne Lanzarini. 1999. *Les nouvelles figures du sous-prolétariat*, Paris:L'Harmattan.

Bruneteaux, Patrick. 2006. "L'hébergement d'urgence à Paris ou l'accueil en souffrance." *Sociétés contemporaines* 3/63: 105-125.

Bruneteaux, Patrick. 2007. "Les politiques de l'urgence à l'épreuve d'une ethnobiographie d'un SDF." *Revue française de sciences politiques* 1/57:47-67.

Burgelin, Jean-François, ed. 2005. *Santé, justice et dangerosités : pour une meilleure prévention de la récidive*. Rapport de la commission Santé-Justice. Paris: La Documentation française.

Burricand Carine, Monteil Marie-Laure. 1996. "Les condamnations pour infraction aux mœurs de 1984 à 1993", *Infostat justice* n°44.

Canivet, Guy, ed. 2000. *L'amélioration du contrôle extérieur des établissements pénitentiaires*. Paris: La Documentation française.

Carlier, Christian. 1996. *Les surveillants au parloir*. Paris: Les éditions de l'atelier.

Carra, Cécile. 1996. "Délinquances juvéniles et régulations institutionnelles." *Droit et Société* 32:105-13.

Carrier, Nicolas. 2010. "Anglo-Saxon Sociologies of the Punitive Turn." *Champ pénal / Penal field*. http://champpenal.revues.org/7818.

Carrier Nicolas and Gilles Chantraine. 2009. "'For' and 'Against' Criminology", *Champ pénal/Penal field*. http://champpenal.revues.org/7422.

Castel, Robert. 2003. *L'insécurité sociale*. Paris:Seuil.

Chantraine, Gilles and Dan Kaminski. 2007. "Rights in Prison. Institutional police, juridical activism, democratic struggle." *Champ pénal/Penal Field,* Séminaire Innovations pénales: http://champpenal.revues.org/document2581.html.

Chantraine, Gilles, and Jean-François Cauchie. 2007. "Entre réalisme et constructivisme, les états épistémologiques du risque", In *Les ambivalences du risque. Regard croisés en sciences sociales*, edited by Yves Cartuyvels, 65-94. Bruxelles: FUSL.

Chantraine, Gilles, Kuhn, André, Mary, Philippe and Marion Vacheret. 2007. "L'Etat en retrait ? 30 ans d'usage de la peine (Belgique, Canada, France, Suisse)." *Déviance et société* 31/4:505-26.

Chantraine, Gilles, ed. 2008. *Trajectoires d'enfermement. Récits de vie au quartier mineurs*. CESDIP: Études & Données Pénales, 106.

Chantraine, Gilles (ed), with Nicolas Sallée, David Scheer, Grégory Salle, Abraham Franssen and Gaëtan Cliquennois. 2011. *Les prisons pour mineurs. Controverses sociales, pratiques professionnelles, expériences de réclusion*, rapport pour la mission de recherche Droit et Justice. CLERSE.

Chantraine, Gilles. 2006. "La prison post-disciplinaire." *Déviance et Société,* 30/3:273-288.

Chantraine, Gilles. 2004. *Par-delà les murs. Expériences et trajectoires en maison d'arrêt*. Paris: Presses universitaires de France/Le Monde.

Chantraine, Gilles. 2009a. "The Post-Disciplinary Prison." In *Discipline, Security and Beyond. Rethinking Michel Foucault 1978 & 1979 Collège de France Lectures,* edited by Bernard Harcourt, 55-76. Chicago: Carceral Notebooks.

Chantraine, Gilles. 2009b. "Juveniles in Detention: Narratives from Prison and Imprisoned Narratives." *Penal Issues* 22/2: http://www.cesdip.fr/spip.php?article437.

Chauvenet Antoinette, Rostaing, Corinne and Françoise Orlic. 2008. *La violence carcérale en question*. Paris: Presses universitaires de France.

Chauvenet, Antoinette. 2010. " 'Les prisonniers': construction et déconstruction d'une notion." *Pouvoirs* 135:41-52.

Chauvin, Sébastien. 2010. *Les agences de la précarité, journaliers à Chicago*. Paris: Seuil.

Christie, Nils, 1981, *Limits to pain*, Oxford: Martin Robertson.

Christie, Nils. 1993. *Crime Control As Industry: Towards Gulags, Western Style ?*. New York: Routledge.

Christie, Nils. 2003. *L'Industrie de la punition. Prison et politique pénale en Occident*. Paris: Autrement.

Christin, Angèle. 2008. *Comparutions immédiates, enquête sur une pratique judiciaire*. Paris: La Découverte.

Cliquennois, Gaëtan. 2006. "Vers une gestion des risques légitimante dans les prisons françaises." In *Prisons et mutations pénales, Déviance et Société*, special issue edited by Gilles Chantraine and Philippe Mary. 3: 355-71.

Cliquennois, Gaëtan. 2009. "Tri et affectation des détenus en régime différencié." *Sociologie du travail* 1:78-96.

Cohen, Stanley. 1985. *Visions of Social Control, crime punishment and classification*. Cambridge: Polity Press.

Collectif. 1977. "La libération conditionnelle." *Actes, cahiers d'actions juridiques* 13-14:66-7.

Comité d'orientation restreint de la loi pénitentiaire (COR). 2007. *Orientations et préconisations*. Paris: La Documentation française.

Comité européen de prévention de la torture (CPT). 2004a. *Rapport au Gouvernement de la République française relatif à la visite effectuée en France par le Comité européen pour la prévention de la torture et des peines ou traitements dégradants du 11 au 17 juin 2003*. Strasbourg: www.cpt.coe.int/fr/etats/fra.htm.

Comité européen de prévention de la torture (CPT). 2004b. *Réponse du gouvernement de la République française au rapport du Comité européen pour la prévention de la torture et des peines ou traitements inhumains ou dégradants (CPT) relatif à sa visite effectuée en France du 11 au 17 juin 2003*. Strasbourg: www.cpt.coe.int/fr/etats/fra.htm.

Commission nationale consultative des droits de l'homme (CNCDH). 2007a. *Sanctionner dans le respect des droits de l'homme, tome 1 : Les droits de l'homme dans la prison*. Paris: La Documentation française.

Commission nationale consultative des droits de l'homme (CNCDH). 2007b. *Sanctionner dans le respect des droits de l'homme, t.2, les alternatives à la détention*. Paris: La Documentation française.

Commission nationale de déontologie de la sécurité (CNDS). 2005. *Rapport 2004*. Paris: La Documentation française.

Conseil de l'Europe. 1999. *Recommandation R(99)22 concernant le surpeuplement des prisons et l'inflation carcérale*. Conseil de l'Europe.

Conseil de l'Europe. 2009. *Questions pénitentiaires : conventions, recommandations et résolutions du Conseil de l'Europe*. Strasbourg: Editions du Conseil de l'Europe.

Contrôleur général des lieux de privation de liberté. 2009. *Rapport de visite de la maison d'arrêt de Lyon-Corbas*. http://www.cglpl.fr/wp-content/uploads/2011/01/MA-Lyon-Corbas-version-web.pdf.

Coye, Stéphanie. 2007. "Leçons finlandaises." *Dedans dehors* 60: 27-28.

Crewe, Ben. 2009. *The Prisoner Society. Power, Adaptation and Social Life in an English Prison*. Clarenton: Clarenton Studies in Criminology.

Damon, Julien. 2002. *La question SDF*. Paris: Presses universitaires de France.

Damon, Julien. 2003. "Cinq variables historiques caractéristiques de la prise en charge des 'SDF'." *Déviance et Société* 27/1:26-27.

Davis, Angela. 2003. *Are Prisons Obsolete ?*. London: Turnaroud Publisher Services ltd.

Davreux, Stéphane *et al.*. 1996. "Le pouvoir pénitentiaire en question(s)" In *Approches de la prison*, edited by Claude Faugeron, Antoinette Chauvenet and Philippe Combessie, 127-150. Paris: De Boeck et Larcier.

Dayant, Charles. 1972. *J'étais médecin à la Santé*. Paris: Presses de la Cité.

Declerck, Patrick. 2001. *Les naufragés, avec les clochards de Paris*. Paris: Plon.

Delmas-Marty, Mireille. 1986. *Le flou du droit*. Paris: Presses universitaires de France.

Direction de l'administration pénitentiaire. 2007. *Projet de Loi pénitentiaire, Comité d'Orientation, Enjeux*. Unpublished manuscript.

Dreyfus, Hubert and Paul Rabinow. 1982. *Michel Foucault. Beyond structuralism and hermeneutics*. Chicago: University of Chicago Press.

Dubret, Gérard. 2005. "Les UHSA, une fausse bonne idée." In *Santé et prison, dix ans après la loi, quelles* évolutions ?, edited by INPES, http://www.inpes.sante.fr/30000/pdf/Actes_Colloque_sante_prison.pdf.

Ewald, François. 1991. "Insurance and Risk", In *The Foucault Effect. Studies in Gouvernmentality*, edited by Graham Burchell, Colin Gordon and Peter Miller, 197-210. Chicago: The University of Chicago Press.

Expertise psychiatrique pénale. 2007. *Rapport de la commission d'audition*. Paris: Haute autorité de santé.

Farges, Eric. 2007. "Penser la réforme pénitentiaire avec Michel Foucault. Apports et limites d'une sociologie politique de la loi du 18 janvier 1994." *Raisons Politiques* 25:101-25.

Faugeron, Claude. 1996. "Une théorie de la prison est-elle possible ?" In *Approches de la prison*, edited by Claude Faugeron, Antoinette Chauvenet, Philippe Combessie, 15-42. Paris: De Boeck et Larcier.

Faugeron, Claude. 2002. "Prisons : la fin des utopies", In *L'institution du droit pénitentiaire, enjeux de la reconnaissance de droits aux détenus*, edited by Olivier Schutter and Dan Kaminski, 289-297. Paris:LGDJ.

Faugeron Claude, and Jean-Michel le Boulaire. 1991. 1991. "Prisons et peines de prison : éléments de construction d'une théorie." *Etudes et données pénales* 61.

Faugeron, Claude and Jean-Michel Le Boulaire. 1992. "Prisons, peines de prisons et ordre public." *Revue française de sociologie* 33/1: 3-32.

Fellner, Jamie. 2005. "Sécurité maximale, le (contre) – modèle américain." *Dedans dehors* 19-20.

Flahault Erika and Dominique Loiseau. 2008. 2008. "Que fait le salariat au militantisme dans les associations féministes ?" *Amnis, revue de civilisation européenne.* 8: http://amnis.revues.org/617.

Foucault, Michel. 1977. *Discipline and Punish: The Birth of the Prison.* New York: Pantheon Books.

Foucault, Michel. 1994 [1977]. "Le poster de l'ennemi public n° 1", In *Dits et écrits*, 256. Paris: Gallimard.

Foucault, Michel. 2001a. "Contre les peines de substitution." *Dits et Ecrits, II, 1976-1988*, 1025. Paris: Gallimard.

Foucault, Michel. 2001b. "Le sujet et le pouvoir"", in *Dits et écrits II, 1976-1988*, 1041-1062. Paris: Gallimard.

Foucault, Michel. 2008. *Psychiatric Power: Lectures at the College de France, 1973-1974.* New York: Palgrave Macmillan.

Fréminville, Bernard de. 1977. *La Raison du plus fort ou petit inventaire des moyens de thérapeutique et de coercition physique imaginés et mis en œuvre par les aliénistes du XIXe siècle comme marque de la prise d'un pouvoir absolu sur le corps des malades.* Paris: Seuil.

Froment, Jean-Charles. 1998. *La République des surveillants de prison, ambiguïté et paradoxes d'une politique pénitentiaire en France.* Paris: LGDJ.

Gaboriau, Patrick and Daniel Terrolle. 2007. *SDF, critique du prêt-à-penser.* Toulouse: Privat.

Garcia, Margarida. 2009. *"Le rapport paradoxal entre les droits de la personne et le droit criminel : les théories de la peine comme obstacles cognitifs à l'innovation"*, PhD diss., Université du Québec à Montréal (UQAM).

Gardella, Edouard. 2001. "Au-delà des lectures sociologiques et psychiatriques de l'exclusion ? À propos des *Naufragés* de Patrick Declerck." *Terrains et Travaux* 2/5:165-76.

Garland, David. 1996. "The limits of the sovereign state: Strategies of crime control in contemporary society." *British Journal of Criminology* 36:445-71.

Garland, David. 2002. *The Culture of Control. Crime and Social Order in Contemporary Society.* Chicago :University Of Chicago Press.

Gaucher, Robert, eds. 2002. *Writing as resistance: the Journal of prisoners on prisons anthology (1988-2002).* Toronto; Canadian Scholars' Press.

Gaucher, Robert. 1988. "The Prisoner as Ethnographer : The Journal of Prisoners on Prisons?"*Journal of Prisoners on Prisons*, 1-1.

Gerald, Niles, 1999. *A Decade of Diesel Therapy in the Floriduh Gulag*, by, Journal of Prisoners on Prisons, Vol. 10 Number 1 & 2

Gibert, Claude. 2003. "La fabrique des risques." *Cahiers internationaux de Sociologie* CXIV:52-72.

Gilbert, Jeremiah. 2009. "'The Same as a Death Sentence': Juvenile Life without Parole."*Journal of Prisoners on Prisons*, 18/1-2.

Goffman, Erving. 1961. *Asylums: Essays on the Social Situation of Mental Patients and Other Inmates*. New York: Doubleday.

Goldman, Pierre. 1975. *Souvenirs obscurs d'un juif polonais né en France*. Paris: Seuil.

Gonin, Daniel. 1967. *Psychothérapie de groupe du délinquant adulte en milieu pénitentiaire*. Paris: Masson.

Gottschalk, Marie. 2006. *The Prison and the Gallows: The Politics of Mass Incarceration in America*. Cambridge: Cambridge University Press.

Goujon, Philippe and Charles Gautier. 2006. *Les délinquants dangereux atteints de troubles psychiatriques : comment concilier la protection de la société et une meilleure prise en charge médicale ?* Rapport d'information. Paris: Sénat.

Hachem Samii, Yahyâ. 2005. "Les jeunes et les I.P.P.J. : 'Jusqu'ici tout va bien ?'." In *Protection de la jeunesse. Formes et réformes. Jeugdbescherming. Vormen en hervormingen*, edited by Jenneke Christiaens, Dominique De Fraene and Isabelle Delens-Ravier, 165-176. Bruxelles: Bruylant.

Hannah-Moffat, Kelly. 2005. "Criminogenic needs and the transformative risk subject." *Punishment and Society* 7/1, 2005:29-51.

Hartman, Kenneth E. 2009. "The Other Death Penalty" *Journal of Prisoners on Prisons*, 18/1-2.

Herzog-Evans, Martine. 2009. "La prétendue 'bonne partie' de la loi pénitentiaire.", *Actualité juridique, Pénal* 12:483-90.

Herzog-Evans, Martine. 2010. "Loi pénitentiaire n° 2009-1436 du 24 novembre 2009 : changement de paradigme pénologique et toute puissance administrative.", *Recueil Dalloz*, 1:31-39.

Hobsbawn, Eric. 1993. "Un historien et son temps présent." In *Ecrire l'histoire du temps présent. En hommage à François Bédarida*, edited by Collectif, 95-102. Paris: CNRS éditions.

Hulsman, Louk and Bernat de Celis, Jacqueline. 1982. *Peines perdues : le système pénal en question*. Paris : Centurion.

Hyest, Jean-Jacques and Guy-Pierre Cabanel, eds. 2000. *Prisons : une humiliation pour la République*. Rapport de la commission d'enquête du Sénat sur les prisons. Paris: Sénat.

Ignatieff, Michael. 1978. *A Just Measure of Pain: Penitentiaries in the Industrial Revolution, 1780–1850*. New York: Pantheon Books.

INSEE. 2002. *L'Histoire familiale des détenus*. Paris: Synthèses, Statistique publique.

Inspection générale de l'administration et Inspection des services judiciaires. 1993. *L'emprisonnement prolongé des détenus difficile et dangereux.* Non publié.

Irwin, John. 2001. *The Jail: Managing the Underclass.* Berkeley: University of California Press.

Irwin, John. 2009. *Lifers: Seeking Redemption in Prison.* New York: Routledge.

Israël, Liora. 2009. "Un droit de gauche ?. Rénovation des pratiques professionnelles et nouvelles formes de militantisme des juristes engagés dans les années 1970." *Sociétés contemporaines* 1/73:47-71.

Jacobson, Michael. 2005. *Downsizing Prisons: How to Reduce Crime and End Mass Incarceration.* New York: New York University Press.

Jaspard, Maryse. 2005. *Les violences contre les femmes.* Paris: La Découverte.

Jobard, Fabien and Gilles Chantraine. 2004. "Trajectoires du contrôle." *Vacarme* 29:138-41.

Kensey Annie and Maud Guillonneau. 1998. *Les à-coups Etude statistique des agressions contre le personnel de surveillance à partir de 376 rapport d'incidents.* Paris: Ministère de la Justice. 53.

Kensey, Annie and Pierre Tournier. 2004. "La récidive des sortants de prison." *Cahiers de démographie pénitentiaire* 15.

Kensey, Annie. 2005. "Durée effective des peines perpétuelles." *Cahiers de démographie pénitentiaire* 18.

Kuhn, André. 2000. *Détenus : Combien ? Pourquoi ? Que faire ?* Berne: Haupt.

Lamalice Olivier and Lalande, Pierre. 2006. *La sévérité pénale à l'heure du populisme.* Ministère de la Sécurité publique du Québec.

Lanzarini, Corinne. 2000. *Survivre dans le monde sous-prolétaire.* Paris: Presses universitaires de France.

Lapeyronnie, Didier. 2008. *Ghetto urbain. Ségrégation, violence, pauvreté en France aujourd'hui.* Paris: Robert Laffont.

Lappi-Seppälä, Tapio. 2005. "Baisse de la population pénale : expériences finlandaises à long terme." In *Politique pénale en Europe, bonnes pratiques et exemples prometteurs* edited by Collectif, 147-170. Strasbourg: Editions du Conseil de l'Europe.

Larsen, Mike and Justin Piché. 2010, "The Moving Targets of Penal Abolitionism: ICOPA, Past, Present and Future." *Contemporary Justice Review*, 13/4, 391-410.

Lascoumes, Pierre. 1997, *Elites irrégulières, essai sur la délinquance d'affaires.* Paris: Gallimard.

Lascoumes, Pierre (dir.). 2010. *Favoritisme et corruption à la française. Petits arrangements avec la probité*. Paris, Presses de Sciences Po.

Lascoumes, Pierre and Ghislaine Moreau-Capdevielle. 1976. "Presse et justice pénale, un cas de diffusion idéologique." *Revue française de sciences politiques* 26/1:41-69.

Lascoumes, Pierre. 1986. *Les affaires ou l'art de l'ombre*. Paris:Le Centurion.

Lascoumes, Pierre. 2011. "Savoirs, expertises et mobilisation." In *Savoirs experts et profanes dans la construction des problèmes publics*, edited by Ludivine Damay, Benjamin Duez and Denis Duez, 221-227. Bruxelles:Facultés Universitaires de Saint-Louis.

Lazerges, Christine. 1982. "L'objection dans le droit pénal moderne, à propos de la loi 'Sécurité et liberté'." *Déviance et société* 6/3:227-257.

Le Caisne, Léonore. 2000. *Prison. Une ethnologue en centrale*. Paris:Odile Jacob.

Le Caisne, Léonore. 2008. *Avoir 16 ans en prison*. Paris: Seuil.

Lechien, Marie-Hélène. 2001. "L'impensé d'une loi pénitentiaire." *Actes de la recherche en sciences sociales* 136-137:15-26.

Legrand, Stéphane. 2007. "Foucault et la théorie du groupe insurrectionnel", conférence prononcée à l'Université de Liège, 23 février.

Lévy, René. 2002. "Sociologie et création de la loi pénale." In *Crime et sécurité, l'état des savoirs*, edited by Laurent Mucchielli and Philippe Robert, 67-75. Paris: La Découverte.

Mansuy, Isabelle. 2005. "The Principle of Legality and the Execution of Sentences in France and Germany: Law = Rights?" *Champ pénal / Penal field* 2: http://champpenal.revues.org/397.

Martuccelli, Danilo. 2004. "Figures de la domination." *Revue française de sociologie* 45/3:473-97.

Mary, Philippe. 2006. "La nouvelle loi pénitentiaire, retour sur un processus de réforme." *Courrier hebdomadaire du CRISP* 11/1916.

Mathiesen, Thomas. (2006 [1990]). *Prisons on Trial*. Winchester: Waterside Press, (third edition).

Mathiesen, Thomas. 1998. "Selective incapacitation revisited." *Law and Human Behavior*, 22(4), 455-469.

Mauer, Marc, and the Sentencing Project. 2006. *Race to Incarcerate*. New York: Free Press.

McNeill, Fergus and Beth Weaver. 2010. *Changing lives? Desistance Research and Offender Management*. Glasgow: Universities of Glasgow and Strathclyde.

Méda, Dominique. 2008. "Le revenu de solidarité active en questions." *La vie des idées* http://www.laviedesidees.fr/Le-Revenu-de-Solidarite-Active-en.html.

Melossi, Dario and Pavarini, Massimo. 1981. *The Prison and the Factory*. London:Critical Criminology MacMillan.

Memmi, Dominique. 2008a. "Mai 68 ou la crise de la domination rapprochée." In *Mai-juin 68*, edited by Dominique Damamme, Boris Gobille, Frédérique Matontiand Bernard Pudal, 35-46. Paris: Editions de l'atelier.

Memmi, Dominique. 2008b. "Sortir de la domination rapprochée." *Vacarme* 43, http://www.vacarme.org/article1548.html.

Mermaz Louis and Jacques Floch, eds. 2000. *La France face à ses prisons. Rapport de la commission d'enquête de l'Assemblée nationale sur les prisons*. Paris: La Documentation française.

Milhaud, Olivier. 2009. "Séparer et punir, les prisons françaises : mise à distance et punition par l'espace.", PhD diss., Université de Bordeaux.

Ministère de la Justice. 2009. *Annuaire statistique de la Justice, édition 2008*. Paris: La Documentation française.

Montandon, Cléopâtre and Bernard Crettaz. 1981. *Paroles de gardiens, paroles de détenus. Bruits et silences de l'enfermement*. Paris: L'Harmattan.

Mouazan, Elenn and Hugues de Suremain. 2007. "Hôpital pénitentiaire de Fresnes, un traitement inhumain reconnu et interrompu par le juge." *Dedans dehors* 60 : 36-37.

Mouesca, Gabriel. 2005. "Etat des lieux du cercle vicieux liant pauvreté, exclusions et milieu carcéral." *Pauvreté, exclusions, la prison en question*. Paris: Emmaüs/OIP.

Mucchielli, Laurent. 2008a. "Une société plus violente ? Une analyse socio-historique des violences interpersonnelles en France, des années 1970 à nos jours." *Déviance et Société* 2-32:115-146.

Mucchielli, Laurent. 2008b. "L'évolution des homicides depuis les années, 1970 : analyse statistique et tendance générale." *Questions pénales* 1-4.

Mucchielli, Laurent. 2011a. " "Délinquance roumaine" : une statistique pour fêter l'anniversaire du discours de Grenoble ?" *Vous avez dit sécurité ?*. http://insecurite.blog.lemonde. fr/2011/07/23/delinquance-roumaine-une-statistique-pour-feter-lanniversaire-du-discours-de-nicolas-sarkozy/.

Mucchielli, Laurent. 2011b. "Erreurs et contre-vérités : Claude Guéant est déjà en campagne électorale." *Vous avez dit sécurité ?* http:// insecurite.blog.lemonde.fr/2011/06/20/claude-gueant-est-deja-en-campagne-electorale/.

Observatoire International des Prisons (OIP). 2005. *Rapport sur les conditions de détention*. Paris: La Découverte.

Paugam, Serge. 2005. "Trajectoires d'exclusion." *Dedans dehors* 47: 12.

Perrault, Gilles. 2001. "Encore un effort." *Hommes & Libertés* 116: 54.

Perrot, Michelle. 1975. "Délinquance et système pénitentiaire en France au XIXe siècle." *Annales, Economies, Sociétés, Civilisations* 1: 67-93.

Perrot, Michelle. 1980. "1848, révolution et prisons.", In *L'impossible prison, recherche sur le système pénitentiaire au XIXe siècle*, edited by Michelle Perrot, 277-312. Paris: Seuil.

Perrot, Michelle. 2004. "La bonne prison, naissance et mort d'un mythe." *Dedans dehors* 45 : 11.

Petit, Jacques-Guy. 1998. *Ces peines obscures, la prison pénale en France, 1780-1875*. Paris: Fayard.

Pirès, Alvaro. 1998. "Aspects, traces et parcours de la rationalité pénale moderne", In *Histoire des savoirs sur le crime et la peine. 2/ La rationalité pénale et la naissance de la criminologie*, edited by Christian Debuyst, Françoise Digneffe et Alvaro Pirès, 3-52. Bruxelles: De Boeck Université.

Porquet, Jean-Luc. 2007. *La débine*. Paris: Flammarion.

Pottier, Philippe. 2005. "Approche de la violence en établissement 13 000." In *Violences en prison*, edited by François Courtine and Marc Renneville, 237-58. Paris: GIP/Mission de recherche Droit et Justice.

Prost, Antoine. 1993. "Pour une histoire sociale du temps présent." In *Ecrire l'histoire du temps présent, En hommage à François Bédarida*, edited by Collectif, 355-59. Paris: CNRS éditions.

Quirion, Bastien. 2007. "Les transformations de l'intervention thérapeutique en milieu correctionnel : pérennité de la logique dominante ou innovations pénales ?" *Champ pénal / Penal Field*. http://champpenal.revues.org/document1471.html.

Rancière, Jacques. 1995. *La Mésentente. Politique et Philosophie*. Paris: Galilée.

Rancière, Jacques. 2009. "Le maître ignorant." *Vacarme*. 09.

Renneville, Marc. 2004. *Crime et folie. Deux siècles d'enquêtes médicales et judiciaires*. Paris: Fayard.

Rhodes, Lorna. 1991. *Emptying Beds: The Work of An Emergency Psychiatric Unit*. Berkeley:University of California Press.

Rhodes, Lorna. 2004. *Total Confinment. Madness and Reason in The Maximum Security Prison*. Berkeley:University of California Press.

Robert, Philippe. 1977. "Les statistiques criminelles et la recherché." *Déviance et société* 1/1: 3-28.

Robert, Philippe. 1984. *La Question pénale*. Genève: Droz.

Robert, Philippe. 2002. "Le sentiment d'insécurité." In *Crime et sécurité, l'état des savoirs*, edited by Laurent Mucchielli and Philippe Robert. Paris: La Découverte.

Robert, Philippe. 2005. *La sociologie du crime*. Paris: La Découverte.

Ross, Jeffrey Ian and Stephen C. Richards, eds. 2003. *Convict Criminology*. Belmont: Wadsworth.

Ross, Jeffrey Ian and Stephen C. Richards. 2002. *Behind Bars: Surviving Prison*. Indianapolis: Alpha Books.

Ross, Jeffrey. 2007. "Supermax Prisons." *Society* 44/3:60-64.

Rouillon, Frédéric, Duburq, Anne, Fagnagni, Francis and Bruno Falissard. 2004. *Étude épidémiologique sur la santé mentale des personnes détenues en prison*. Paris: Inserm.

Salle, Grégory and Gilles Chantraine. 2009. "Le droit emprisonné ? Sociologie des usages sociaux du droit en prison." *Politix* 3/87: 93-117.

Salle, Grégory. 2004. "Mettre la prison à l'épreuve. Le GIP en guerre contre l' 'Intolérable'." *Cultures & Conflits* 55: 71-96.

Salle, Grégory. 2007. "Une sociologie des 'taulards' : la convict criminology." *Genèses* 3/68:132-44.

Salle, Grégory. 2009. *La part d'ombre de l'Etat de droit, la question carcérale en France et en République fédérale d'Allemagne depuis 1968*. Paris: Editions de l'EHESS.

Schnapper, Bernard. 1983. "La récidive, une obsession créatrice au 19e siècle." In *Le Récidivisme, XXIe Congrès de l'Association Française de Criminologie*. Paris:PUF.

Scott, James. 1990. *Domination and the arts of résistance*: *Hidden Transcripts*. London, Yale University Press.

Simonnot, Dominique. 2003. *Justice en France, une loterie nationale*. Paris: La Martinière.

Snacken, Sonja. 1997. "Peines de longues durée et délinquants violents." In *Actes de la 12e Conférence des Directeurs d'Administration Pénitentiaire (CDAP)*. Strasbourg: Editions du Conseil de l'Europe.

Soutrenon, Emmanuel. 2005. "Offrons-leur l'asile ! Critique d'une représentation des clochards en 'naufragés'." *Actes de la recherche en sciences sociales* 4:88-115.

Terrolle, Daniel. 2004. "La ville dissuasive: l'envers de la solidarité avec les SDF." *Espaces et sociétés* 1/2:116-117.

Tocqueville, Alexis de. 1984. *Œuvres complètes, tome 4, Ecrits sur le système pénitentiaire en France et à l'étranger*, edited by Michelle Perrot. Paris: Gallimard.

Tonry, Michael, ed. 2001. *Penal Reform in Overcrowded Times*. New York: Oxford University Press.

Tonry, Michael. 1995. *Malign Neglect: Race, Class, and Punishment in America*. New York: Oxford University Press.

Tournier, Pierre-Victor. "La tentative du procureur de Dunkerque pour limiter la surpopulation carcérale. Une décision de bon sens ?" *Arpenter le champ pénal* 235-236.

Tournier, Pierre-Victor. 2011a. "Population des prisons." *Opale-Observatoire national de la délinquance et des réponses pénales* 2: 4-88.

Tournier, Pierre-Victor. 2011b. "Placement sous main de justice dans les SPIP." *Opale-Observatoire national de la délinquance et des réponses pénales*. 2: 104-105.

Tubex, Hilde, Snacken, Sonja. 1996. "L'évolution des longues peines de prison : sélectivité et dualisation." In *Approches de la prison*, edited by Claude Faugeron, Antoinette Chauvenet, Philippe Combessie, 222-43. Paris: De Boeck et Larcier.

Tulkens, Françoise. 2001. "L'individualisation de la peine, cent ans après Saleilles." In *L'individualisation de la peine, de Saleilles à aujourd'hui*, edited by Reynald Ottenthof. Paris: Erès.

Tulkens, Françoise. 2006. "L'extension du domaine de droits." *Dedans-Dehors* 54:24-25.

Union syndicale des magistrats (USM). 2000. *Livre blanc sur l'exécution des peines*. http://usm2000.free.fr/article.php3?id_article=29.

Van den Boogaard, Claire. 2010. "Apprendre ou à laisser." *Passe-Murailles* 22:12-14.

Vasseur, Véronique. 2000. *Médecin-chef à la prison de la Santé*. Paris: Le Cherche Midi.

Wacquant, Loïc. 2001. "Deadly symbiosis, When ghetto and prison meet and mesh." *Punishment & Society* 3/1:95-134.

Wacquant, Loïc. 2009. *Punishing the Poor: The Neoliberal Government of Social Insecurity*. Durham: Duke University Press.

Wacquant, Loïc. 2010a. "Class, race & hyperincarceration in revanchist America." *Daedalus* 139/3:74–90.

Wacquant, Loïc. 2010b. "Prisoner reentry as myth and ceremony." *Dialectical Anthropology* 34/4:605-20.

Zedner, Lucia. 2007. "Pre-crime and post-criminology." *Theoretical criminology* 11/2:261-81.

APPENDIX 1
Statistics on the French carceral population

Source: (Tournier 2011a), available on http://www.inhesj.fr/ fichiers/ondrp/opale/opale2.pdf (in French).

1. EVOLUTION OF THE CARCERAL POPULATION, 1970-2010.

The carceral population [population écrouée] includes people in detention, people wearing electronic bracelets, or under specific types of incarceration such as semi-release.

1/1/70	1/1/72	1/1/74	1/1/76	1/1/78	1/1/80	1/1/82	1/1/84	1/1/86	1/1/88
29 026	31 668	27 100	29 482	32 259	35 655	30 340	38 634	42 617	49 328

1/1/90	1/1/92	1/1/94	1/1/96	1/1/98	1/1/00	1/1/02	1/1/04	1/1/06	1/1/08	1/1 10
43 913	48113	50 240	52 658	50 744	48 049	45 319	55 355	59 522	64 003	66 089

2. THE NUMBER OF PEOPLE PLACED UNDER CONSTANT ELECTRONIC SURVEILLANCE, 2007-2011

1/1/07	1/1/08	1/1/09	1/1/10	1/1/11
1 648	2 506	3431	4489	5 767

3. THE NUMBER OF DETAINED PERSONS SERVING A LONG SENTENCE (FIVE YEARS OR MORE), 1975-2010.

1/1/75	1/1/80	1/1/85	1/1/90	1/1/95	1/1/00	1/1/05	1/1/10
3 332	5 324	5 989	8 256	10 228	12 841	14 039	13 442

APPENDIX 2
Presidents, Prime Ministers and Ministers of Justice in France (1981-2012)

The periods 1993-1995 and 1997-2002 are periods of political "cohabitation" (the President's political party differs from that of the National Assembly and the government).

Presidents	François Mitterrand (1981-1988), left		François Mitterrand (1988-1995), left	
Prime Ministers	Pierre Mauroy (1981-1984) left Laurent Fabius (1984-1986), left	Jacques Chirac (1986-1988), right	Michel Rocard (1988-1991), left Edith Cresson 1991-1992), left Pierre Bérégovoy (1992-1993), left	Edouard Balladur (1993-1995), right
Ministers of Justice	Robert Badinter (1981-1986), left	Albin Chalandon (1986-1988), right	Pierre Arpaillange (1988-1990), left Henri Nallet (1990-1992), left Michel Vauzelle (1992-1993), left	Pierre Méhaignerie (1993-1995), right

Presidents	Jacques Chirac (1995-2002), right		Jacques Chirac (2002-2007), right	Nicolas Sarkozy (2007-), right
Prime Ministers	Alain Juppé (1995-1997), right	Lionel Jospin (1997-2002), left	Jean-Pierre Raffarin (2002-2005), right Dominique de Villepin (2005-2007), right	François Fillon (2007-), right
Ministers of Justice	Jacques Toubon (1995-1997), right	Elizabeth Guigou (1997-2000), left Marylise Lebranchu (2000-2002), left	Dominique Perben (2002-2005), right Pascal Clément (2005-2007), right	Rachida Dati (2007-2009), right Michèle Alliot-Marie (2009-2010), right Michel Mercier (2010-2012)

www.ingramcontent.com/pod-product-compliance
Lightning Source LLC
Chambersburg PA
CBHW020353270326
41926CB00007B/412